CHESAPEAKE 1850

STEAMBOATS AND OYSTER WARS - The Newsreader

KEN ROSSIGNOL

**The Privateer Clause Publishing Co. /
THE CHESAPEAKE TODAY LLC**

Copyright © 2012 Kenneth C. Rossignol / The Privateer Clause Publishing Co, / THE CHESAPEAKE TODAY LLC.

All rights reserved

The characters and events portrayed in this book are fictitious. Any similarity to real persons, living or dead, is coincidental and not intended by the author.

No part of this book may be reproduced, or stored in a retrieval system, or transmitted in any form or by any means, electronic, mechanical, photocopying, recording, or otherwise, without express written permission of the publisher.

ISBN-10 : 1479237906
ISBN-13 : 978-1479237906

Cover design by: Elizabeth Mackey
Printed in the United States of America

www.theprivateerclause.com
ken@theprivateerclause.com
www.titanicspeakersbureau.com

This book is dedicated to the men and women who lived and worked on the Chesapeake Bay steamships and worked the water on vessels of all types.

When the crabs of the Chesapeake have soft shells, we ensnare them, fry them and feast upon them. When their shells grow hard, we boil them and feast upon them. When they disappear we turn to the oyster, and between times we nourish our systems with the strawberry, the Ann Aranel watermelon, the cantaloupe, the diamondback terrapin, corn on the cob, tomatoes, Blue Mountain peaches, smelts, corncakes, turkeys and canvasback ducks. Maryland is always well fed. Hence the beauty of its women and the noble presence and flashing eyes of its men.

The largest genuine Maryland oyster—the veritable bivalve of the Chesapeake...is as large as your open hand. A magnificent, matchless reptile! Hard to swallow? Dangerous? Perhaps to the novice, the dastard. But to the veteran of the raw bar, the man of trained and lusty esophagus, a thing of prolonged and kaleidoscopic flavors, a slow sipping saturnalia, a delirium of joy!

H. L. MENCKEN

CONTENTS

Title Page
Copyright
Dedication
Epigraph
Introduction
SKIPJACKS
One - A Day on the Bay 5
Two - A Night in a Hurricane 10
Three – Honest Point Store 17
Four – A Midsummer Night's Dream 22
Five – The Hanging 30
Six – Nomini and a New Friend 35
Seven – Slaves for Sale 42
Eight - Shore Mayhem 47
Nine - A New Job 52
Ten - Marrying Molly 61
Eleven - War on the Chesapeake and Potomac 68

Twelve - Frozen Rivers to Big Changes	92
Thirteen – Death of a President	105
Fourteen - Good Fortunes	110
Fifteen -The Fourth and Family Affairs	114
Sixteen - Renewed Oyster War on the Bay	119
Seventeen - A Sunday Picnic	125
Eighteen – A New Line	130
MORE BOOKS BY KEN ROSSIGNOL	147
About The Author	151
Books By This Author	153

INTRODUCTION

Life on the Chesapeake Bay region in this book is accurately described to the best of the author's knowledge, drawing on a lifetime of living in the area. The history of the United States is also presented with adherence to authentic events. The story of the Douglas family, while fictional, parallels that of many families in the Chesapeake Bay tidewater region.

Acknowledgments

The publications cited in this book are actual, as are the events described in the reporting of the time. The excellent work of the Library of Congress in preserving these memories and the history of the nation was invaluable in creating this book.

SKIPJACKS

The Maryland General Assembly passed a law in 1865 that prohibited vessels powered by engines from the use of dredges to harvest oysters. Skipjacks relied only on sail power to work the Chesapeake Bay and thus were allowed to dredge for oysters.

Available In Kindle, Paperback,

Hardcover, And Audible At Amazon And Retailers Worldwide

Additional books by Ken Rossignol

Chesapeake 1850
Chesapeake 1880
Chesapeake 1910

True Crime

MURDER USA: True Crime, Real Killers
MURDER CHESAPEAKE: True Crime, Real Killers
CHESAPEAKE TRUE CRIME - Top Stories from The Chesapeake Today

Twentieth Century History

SPANISH INFLUENZA - The Story of the Epidemic That Swept America From the Newspaper Reports of 1918
Panama 1914 The Early Years of the Big Dig
Titanic 1912 The original news reporting of the sinking of the Titanic
Titanic & Lusitania- Survivor Stories (with Bruce M.Caplan)
Titanic Poetry, Music & Stories
KLAN: Killing America
Leopold & Loeb Killed Bobby Franks (with Bruce

M. Caplan)
SINS OF HER FATHER: Pelosi's Pop Liked Racists and Had High Praise for Fascist Mussolini

Battle of Solomon's Island
The Story of The Rag
Cheap Shots: THE EDITORIAL CARTOONS OF ST. MARY'S TODAY: The Story of The Rag

The Chesapeake Short Stories Collection

The Chesapeake: Tales & Scales (with Larry Jarboe)
The Chesapeake: Legends, Yarns & Barnacles (with Larry Jarboe)
The Chesapeake: Oyster Buyboats, Ships & Steamed Crabs
THE CHESAPEAKE: A Man Born to Hang, Can Never Drown
THE CHESAPEAKE: Country Cornpone Cornucopia
THE CHESAPEAKE: Tidewater Sagas

Cruising the Waterfront Restaurants of the Potomac
Coke Air: Chesapeake Crime Confidential
Pirate Trials: Dastardly Deeds & Last Words
Pirate Trials: Hung by the Neck Until Dead
Pirate Trials: Famous Murderous Pirates Book

Series: THE LIVES AND ADVENTURES of FAMOUS and SUNDRY PIRATES

PIRATE TRIALS: The Three Pirates - Famous Murderous Pirate Books Series: The Islet of the Virgin

The Traveling Cheapskate Series:

The Ninety-Nine Cent Tour of Bar Harbor Maine

Boating Chesapeake Bay

Fire Cruise

Enter Today With Your Email Address For A Chance To Win A Free Paperwhite Kindle Or Fire Tablet

Visit ThePrivateerClause.com and submit your name and email address and win a free Kindle book along with a chance to win a tremendous new Paperwhite.

Steamboat Days

A steamer on the Appomattox River.
Library of Congress.

ONE - A DAY ON THE BAY

The steamboat Savannah was making good time, with calm seas and little wind as it left Norfolk, heading for Washington, then to Baltimore. We were on the first leg of a trip that would see the fine twenty-year-old ship visit dozens of wharves along the way.

I watched as my grandfather stood next to the helm, keeping a careful eye on old Willy at the wheel and glancing over his shoulder as storm clouds continued to build in the south.

The *Savannah* worked its way into shallows and edged carefully up to dock at wharves along the western shore of the Chesapeake on the tenth day of June 1850. Milford Haven, a small bay, led us to Marchant's Wharf, where we loaded the season's first crop of watermelons and tomatoes, which we would take to Washington and Baltimore.

Tasting the bright red tomatoes was one of my privileges as a cabin boy assigned to my grandpa, the captain. It was a task I was happy to perform—giving Grandpa a proper report, pronouncing the vegetables prime for the market, not that my opinion on their fitness mattered much. Because my pay was but a dollar a week, food was a big consideration as compensation for my work.

After leaving Marchant's Wharf, the *Savannah* crossed Milford Haven to Hickory Cove to take on ten crates of noisy chickens and two cows. With room for only fifty passengers, the real business purpose of the ship was to carry freight and various goods to market from the many farms and wharves along the Chesapeake.

Since reaching the age of ten, I worked with my grandpa after school let out in mid-April. My choices were to work on my uncle's farm in Georgia or work on the water with Grandpa. Not much of a choice at all for a lad who wanted adventure.

Life as a farmhand held no promise of meeting pirates but only of being introduced to boll weevils.

Had I possessed the money, I would surely have paid the Norfolk and Baltimore Line a dollar a week just to travel along with my grandfather. School was a bother, and working on the steamboat was great fun, even though it traveled far from home.

The *Savannah* had been sold by Georgia & Carolina Company after it took delivery of two new coastal steamships. The new ships didn't have a stern paddle wheel, but side-wheels, which were said to be easier to navigate.

When the *Savannah* was sent north to Virginia, Grandpa was part of the deal. My father had died the previous winter after a bout of pneumonia, and Grandpa decided that I needed a lot of watching. My mother was busy with five younger children, so it was to sea with me... even if just 'til fall, when school started again.

The *Savannah* could handle rough weather, which was lucky, as thunderstorms came up most every afternoon; they would suddenly pop up from the west and strike out across the wide bay. Grandpa was experienced at running a steamboat. Sixty-four years old, he had been working on ships since he was my age. Most every day, when clouds started to build from the west side of the bay, he would find a safe harbor or pull up to one of the wharves we had previously visited along the way and wait out the storm, which usually vented its fury in less than a half-hour. Then we would be on our way again.

After Grandpa and Willy steered the large ship out of the shallow cove and past a point mysteriously named "Hole in the Wall," we began to steam out into the open bay on our way to Deltaville.

Another fifteen minutes passed, and soon we rounded the point at Gwynn. We made one more stop at a farm wharf marked only by a shed on shore with a sign nailed to it with the word Grimstead painted on it.

Three more stops, at Cobbs Creek, Watson Creek, and Horse Point, began to fill the freight deck with more bushels of tomatoes and crates of chickens, geese, and a dozen hogs. Until the livestock settled down, we had quite a symphony to entertain the passengers. As long as the ship was underway, most of the animal smells trailed off behind it, but if the wind blew from aft, the ship took on the smells of a farmyard.

Finally, it was time to stop at Deltaville, which was a fine village. With two churches, a large general store at the end of the wharf, a full block of shops, and a café, it was one of just a few small towns along the way north to Washington, D.C. All the rest of our stops were just wharves at the end of farm roads. A line of hogsheads of tobacco and wagon loads of produce were usually waiting for us at our stops, but at Deltaville, where we would linger for up to a half-hour, a lad like me had a chance to wander around and gawk at a new world.

Grandpa kept looking over his shoulder to the south at the clouds on the horizon.

We hadn't had a thunderstorm that day, and Grandpa was even more worried when the brief storms never arrived from the west.

"Willy, we have to get out of Deltaville and get back around the point into the Rappahannock River as quick as we can. Keep the speed up and, without coming too close to the point, let's hurry around to a safe harbor," Grandpa said. "I can't help but feel that those clouds from the south spell trouble for us."

"Captain, there is a nice spot at Mason's Cove, just before Grey's Point, where we can hole up," Willy offered.

"That's where we will head, my boy. We can hide from this storm there and then make it to Weems, where we can tie up for the night."

"Captain, I think this storm might blow hard and long, and we might have to stay over right there in that cove."

"Be that as it may, Willy, just keep her strong on course for Mason's Cove, and I will tell the crew to get everything battened down good. I don't want us to lose any cargo during the storm."

When Grandpa left the wheelhouse, it gave me the opportunity to climb into his seat and watch the bay churn up in front of us as Willy guided the ship into the Rappahannock River.

TWO - A NIGHT IN A HURRICANE

The late-June hurricane swept up the Atlantic coast and blew in over Virginia, with a fury best never experienced up close. I knew from listening to Willy's stories that my grandpa, Captain Douglas, had seen more than a few such storms over the years, and that experience led him to carefully choose his spot in Mason's Cove to ride out the storm.

A strong farm wharf with large pilings, it

served more than a dozen farms and a few large plantations. The wharf presented a secure shelter for the *Savannah* against the ravages of the strong winds. The crew worked fast and, using every foot of heavy lines on the ship, tied her fast to the dock. Strong rain came with the winds, and a drenching rain pounded the Savannah for four hours before letting up.

As Grandpa kept an eye on the storm and the ship, the severe weather suddenly slackened.

"Looks like it's all done, Grandpa!"

"Ethan, this is just the calm as the eye of the storm passes over. Then it will come back and hit us harder than before. Help Willy go around and check all the lines, and tighten the hatch cover over the freight hold."

As the night came over them and the wind roared back to full hurricane strength, the passengers sat around the main salon of the *Savannah,* careful to stay away from the windows. A tree came crashing down from shore and landed on the starboard side of the big boat, one branch shattering a window. Broken glass flew across the salon, luckily missing those who were cowering from the storm.

The crewmen kept pumping the bailing hoses as water filled the bilges as fast as they could pump them. I was too small to take a turn on the large handle running the bilge pump, and for once, I was glad to be sidelined for a task. The big Irishman called Fitz worked a pump for five minutes, and then O'Brien took a turn. They would cuss each other's effort and laugh as the other slowed down and needed a break. This went on for another four hours before the rain and winds let up. I watched in fascination as the men sweated and swore and kept the storm water from building up in the engine room.

When the sun rose over the Chesapeake and brightened up Mason's Cove, Captain Douglas took a look out of the pilothouse and surveyed the damage. The *Savannah* had come out of the storm in good shape—one tree tossed onto the boat and a broken window. Branches were scattered across the boat's starboard side, which was closest to shore, and a small rowboat had been blown up onto the bow. Captain Douglas walked onto the forward deck and noted that the rowboat was in good shape. He ordered two deckhands to move it to the wharf where the owner might find it.

The way out of Mason's Cove was clear, with the exception of a twenty-four-foot bugeye that had broken loose from its mooring and was floating clear. A gentle nudge from the side of the *Savannah* would push it out of the way. I walked along behind my grandpa as he inspected the ship and ordered the crew to prepare to make way.

"Lad, now that you see how to survive a major blow from a hurricane see if you can help the cook get breakfast ready. I am sure our passengers are starving, but first, bring your grandfather a big cup of coffee to the wheelhouse. Now, be off with you."

"Yes, Grandpa, right away." I hurried down to the galley and quickly returned with his coffee.

Then it was back to work with Mrs. Langley, our jolly cook, who liked my help in the kitchen and made sure I was well fed. Peeling potatoes was but a prelude to dining delights; I could eat at least three of her big crab cakes, along with a half-dozen ears of sweet corn slathered with fresh butter. I was also allowed the special joy of listening to Mrs. Langley sing as she bustled about the galley preparing meals. Great food and free entertainment, how could life be any better? It would be painful to return to school in late October and leave life on the water behind.

The *Savannah* traveled fairly slowly as it picked its way into wharves and village docks to pick up people and freight on the way to Baltimore. A few peddlers who had boarded in Norfolk would leave the ship with bulging packs and spend the day in a village, making their rounds selling their wares and then boarding once more before we left. If the peddlers were doing well, they might spend time walking to nearby farms and plantations and catch the boat the following week to return to Norfolk.

The day following, the fury unfurled by the hurricane found the sky crisp and blue, and the Rappahannock littered with parts of boats, sheds, duck blinds, and a few floating corpses—animal and human.

The *Savannah* made more than twenty stops as it headed to the town of Tappahannock before its return trip downriver. All hands, crew, and passengers solemnly watched as boats picked up the bodies of at least six deceased who had been caught out in the storm.

At some stops, the freight to be shipped to Baltimore had been destroyed by the big storm; at others, which were sheltered from the wind, there was no damage.

I spent the day going back and forth from the wheelhouse to the galley, helping Mrs. Langley prepare her meals for the passengers, and taking lunch and coffee to Willy and Grandpa. Neither of them left their duty all day unless we were stopped at a wharf. One of my chief duties was to pick crabs and dig out the meat from the claws and bodies of the bright red creatures after they were steamed. Mrs. Langley used the meat for her rich and hearty crab soup and for her delicious crab cakes. That I was assigned as her chief and principal crab picker gave me an easy way to get my fill of the sweet and delicious meat. Her large container of Baltimore spice—used for cooking the pot of scrambling blue crabs, which seemed to be on the big stove every day—would be depleted by the time we got to the city. Another big keg of crab spice would be loaded, along with other goods for delivery to the farms and towns along our way.

I didn't want to even think about what I would do without my daily diet of crab cakes come fall.

My other duty was that of cleaning fish. Mrs. Langley was an expert in this skill, along with all the others required to run the kitchen and dining room of a large steamboat on the Chesapeake.

She schooled me for several days, until I got the hang of stripping the meat of a nice rockfish cleanly off the bones. After putting the rest of the carcass in a pot, she would boil it down and strain out the bones to catch the remainder of the meat for a fish stew. The guts and fish heads went into another large keg, which was sold to men at the wharves for crab bait when we stopped. Nothing was wasted.

The trip to Tappahannock and back down the Rappahannock River—aside from watching the bodies being fished from the river—was uneventful. Willy and Grandpa were not going to let anything happen to the *Savannah*; wrecks of boats and buildings that had blown across the path of the ship during the storm were carefully avoided. We were quickly out on the open waters of the Chesapeake and headed north to Reedville, then back out in the bay and around to Smith Point.

"Boy, we are now in Maryland waters. Sometimes these Virginia lads and the roughnecks from Maryland get to shooting each other over what they call the 'white gold,' the great numbers of oysters brought up from the beds in the water," Grandpa explained. "They usually aren't any problem for us, as we carry a great deal of supplies they need for their families, but it doesn't hurt to keep a sharp eye out for trouble in these parts."

Willy laughed and said the watermen have warred for years over oyster rights and even mounted cannon on their boats to sink their enemies, just like the pirates of old. I thought Willy might be exaggerating, but Grandpa nodded.

"He's telling the truth, lad. These oystermen can be deadly when it comes to others poaching their oyster beds. We are now on the Potomac, and from here on, we maintain a constant watch. You can bring your 'taters and crabs to the forward deck and keep an eye out while you get your chores done for Mrs. Langley. And don't eat so much of the crab meat that she won't have any for crab cakes," Grandpa said with a laugh.

Unloading the freight

THREE – HONEST POINT STORE

Going up the Potomac, Willy steered the Savannah over to the Virginia side, and the ship entered a bay he called "the Glebe." Willy did not know why it had that name. The steamboat slowed and carefully came alongside a wharf with a general store built high up on the shore, away from flood tides, with a sign that read Honest Point Store.

Grandpa told me that I could get out on land

and run around because we would be there about two hours as the crew loaded up freight that had been stored in a sturdy warehouse behind the store. The cove was similar to Mason's Cove, where the *Savannah* had been holed up, and it had also escaped any serious damage.

"We might see the Maryland side tore up a lot more," Grandpa said.

"Captain Douglas, do I have time to walk over to my cousin's farm? It's just down the road a piece," Willy said.

"Why don't you go in the store and ask Mr. Miller if you can borrow one of his horses? I don't want to be sitting here wondering when you will be back."

Willy nodded and headed into the store to seek permission. A few minutes later, he went out to the stable and saddled up a fine quarter horse, and rode off to his cousin's farm.

"Lad, you take your chances when you let your helmsman quit the boat for any reason. Willy doesn't have a cousin here. It's that widow lady over on the next farm he is going to see. He goes there every time we pull into Honest Point. It appears that the name of the store hasn't rubbed off much on Willy," Grandpa noted with a laugh. "But he always seems to come back, though I have had to sound the whistle a couple of times to remind him to saddle up and get back to the wharf."

I wasn't sure what Willy did for the Widow Jones. I assumed he helped her with her chores—

maybe splitting firewood—though if he was doing that already, he must be expecting a hard winter.

I sat alongside Grandpa as he and Mr. Miller talked about the hurricane. Mr. Miller had spent the storm in his store at Honest Point with his family. Grandpa told him what we had seen on our trip up to the village of Tappahannock. It would be a week or two before they learned who the people were who had been claimed by the storm. The small newspaper in that town would carry the news of the deceased.

The latest stories about the never-ending oyster wars between the Maryland and Virginia watermen dominated the conversation between the men after they got through discussing the storm.

"They had a big shootout last weekend," Mr. Miller said. "Some boys from up at Kinsale were moving up St. George's Creek, past the island over on the Maryland side, at about five o'clock in the morning, and a sloop filled with shooters bushwhacked them. One of the Virginia boys was killed, and several were wounded."

"How many dead does that make this year?" Captain Douglas asked.

"At least a dozen, not that the world might not be better off without some of those characters. Many of them are out stealing whatever they can, instead of doing honest work."

"One of the Keyser boys from Lewisetta was the one killed last month, and his family only has one boy left to work the water," Mr. Miller added.

The storekeeper occasionally waited on a customer, then returned to the bar and his conversation with Grandpa. One of the gamblers on the boat entered the store, apparently looking for a new game because he had wrung the available cash from the willing players on the ship.

"I expect you might be anxious to get to Baltimore?" Grandpa asked.

"Yes, Captain Douglas. The availability of card players on this trip is right slim and darn close to none. An honest man can't make a living on this sailing."

"Where was the honest man?" Mr. Miller asked with a big grin.

"Storekeeper, there is no sign over my head proclaiming 'honest' as there is over your store," Jack Deagle, the gambler, said. "Life on the water is always a gamble; consider the bodies of those poor souls we saw on the Rappahannock after the hurricane."

CHESAPEAKE 1850

Lashed to safety during a storm. F. C. Yohn

FOUR – A MIDSUMMER NIGHT'S DREAM

The Savannah worked its way up the Potomac River, stopping at a few more Virginia wharves, including Coles Point, then crossed the river to the Maryland shore at Piney Point and Tolson's Wharf. More tomatoes were brought aboard; the crop had benefited from an early spring. Sweet corn, fresh fish, oysters, and several bushels of lively crabs filled the freight hold. The ice, which was hard to come by, was used sparingly for the oysters, which would be the last seen until fall.

Willy and Grandpa were alert to the roustabouts at the pier loading the freight as some of the men were drinking. One of the laborers set down his bottle to carry crates of chickens on board; another man knocked it over, spilling the precious spirits. A fight ensued, ending with one of the men wallowed by an uppercut that sent him sprawling backward off the wharf. A lad of my age couldn't ask for better sport than that, and the fisticuffs brightened the day for all of us.

The weather was crystal clear, and since the hurricane two days prior, the daily onslaught of thunderstorms had ceased. The breeze was warm but pleasant, and the *Savannah* continued to travel up the Maryland coastline and to Breton Bay, where more entertainment awaited us.

The *Savannah* pulled into the wharf at Leonardtown, located at the head of Breton Bay, and slid toward the dock, which was already overwhelmed by the huge *James Adams Floating Theatre*. The big ship was basically a barge with an engine and pilot house; it toured small ports on the Chesapeake region, putting on plays and other dramatic productions. I had never seen one and asked my grandpa if we would be staying overnight in Leonardtown so I could attend that night's show.

"Boy, not only do we have a schedule to keep, but the shows they put on in that theatre are not meant for a ten-year-old boy. You might have a few laughs, but much of it would bore you silly," Grandpa said.

"Well, I did enjoy that boxing match on the pier downriver, though it was short-lived," I replied. "Do they have any prize fights in that theatre?"

"No, lad, they put on plays by Shakespeare, such as *Romeo and Juliet* and *Julius Caesar*, but not a single fistfight."

Just as I thought our stay at Leonardtown would not allow me a chance to see a play on the floating theatre, my hopes were renewed. The ship's purser, who handled the collection of fares and freight charges, came to the wheelhouse.

"Captain Douglas, we are only at about half capacity in our cabins right now, and since we arrived, I have had more than thirty people inquire about passage to other stops, but only if we can delay our departure until after ten o'clock tomorrow morning," Frank Abell said.

"Mr. Abell, we would be put behind schedule if we stay overnight here, and I don't know if we can make it up."

"We might be behind in time, Captain, but we won't be behind in money."

"What in the world makes these folks want to stay in this backwater town for another night?"

"They're having themselves a hangin' in the

morn'. We can leave, but these folks said they don't care. Another steamboat will be here in a couple of days, but they ain't gonna miss a hangin'."

"They plan these things here?"

"This one's official. It's at the courthouse on top of the hill, at the hangin' tree. The chap who is going to get his neck stretched ran over the mayor's daughter with his wagon. He was drunk, and it don't help much that he got that way from celebrating his new freedom from being a slave. They say he had been celebrating for a week when he ran over the child and killed her dead."

"Well, it will surely help our books if we take on thirty passengers at one stop. Let the crew know we will remain here tonight and leave promptly at eleven in the morn," the captain said.

"One more thing, Mr. Abell."

"Yes, sir?"

"Arrange for more ice and coal. We might as well stock up while we are here."

"Aye, Captain."

"And make sure you aren't cheated. They have a lot of thieves in this part of the country."

***

My grandpa took me to see the play that night, and I didn't understand too much, just as he'd said.

The billboard at the ticket window read *A Midsummer Night's Dream*, a play by William Shakespeare.

The *James Adams Floating Theatre* held about one hundred fifty people, who all paid the handsome sum of five cents each to watch the play. The ladies were dressed in their Sunday best, and the men wore proper coats and ties. I wondered if they would be as well dressed for the hanging the next morning.

The long barge had two floors that accommodated a large theatre and stage. The actors and actresses were dressed in finery that small towns rarely see. The rows of seats filled up as eight p.m. approached. Large oil lamps lined the walls, and a row of lamps burned along the foot of the stage to light up the actors. This was not an evening to miss in a small town such as Leonardtown.

The actors all spoke in some high-falutin' tone, in a strange dialect that pleased the audience but left us young'uns bewildered.

A few of the men were taking nips of whiskey from their flasks as their wives crested and fell on every sound uttered by the performers. After about an hour and a half, the play ended, and the crowd chattered as the players greeted them as they left the floating theatre.

After we returned to the *Savannah,* I went to the small library on the ship and found *A Midsummer Night's Dream* in a book, and over the next several days, read it over a few times. I found some paper and pen and, for the first time, I put to work some of what I had been learning in school and copied out a passage from the play.

HELENA

Call you me fair? That fair again unsay.

Demetrius loves your fair: O happy fair!
Your eyes are lode-stars; and your tongue's sweet air
More tuneable than lark to shepherd's ear,
When wheat is green, when hawthorn buds appear.
Sickness is catching: O, were favour so,
Yours would I catch, fair Hermia, ere I go;
My ear should catch your voice, my eye your eye,
My tongue should catch your tongue's sweet melody.
Were the world mine, Demetrius being bated,
The rest I'd give to be to you translated.
O, teach me how you look, and with what art
You sway the motion of Demetrius' heart.
> *HERMIA*
> **I frown upon him, yet he loves me still.**
> *HELENA*
> **O that your frowns would teach my smiles such skill!**
> *HERMIA*
> **I give him curses, yet he gives me love.**

That was my first introduction into understanding the world of love among adults. It was a lot for a ten-year-old to comprehend, and the subject never really became any clearer as I aged. I think I would rather have seen a prize fight.

The Steamboat Pocahontas at Norfolk, Virginia

The Steamboat Louisa ran between Baltimore, Maryland, and Fort Monroe in Virginia. Library of Congress

CHESAPEAKE 1850

The steamboat Pocahontas at Norfolk, Va.

FIVE – THE HANGING

John Henry Plater sat in his jail cell, holding his head. It had been aching for a month, ever since the day he had killed that child. At the age of thirty-eight, he had worked all his life for his master and had rejoiced to learn that he would be given his freedom. A life of planting and cutting tobacco, tending livestock, and driving freight down to the steamboat landing at Sotterley Plantation had made his hands hard and his back weak.

Finally, old Judge Plater had taken ill and decided it was time to give ten of his slaves their freedom before he died. That still left another fifty slaves to keep the old place going.

Sotterley sat on a hillside overlooking the Patuxent River, more than five thousand acres of rich farmland sweeping down to the river that hosted vast quantities of oysters, crab, and fish.

John Henry had taken Judge Plater's last name, as most freed slaves had done. When he was told to go to Leonardtown to pick up supplies at the hardware store, he had stopped in at one of the taverns that kept a door open for coloreds. A couple of hours in the dark barroom had left John Henry pretty well liquored up for his drive back to Sotterley.

John Henry was a God-fearing man who was proud of his family, all of whom lived in their own slave quarters on the plantation. His wife and three daughters would soon be moving with him to the cabin he had been given, along with thirty acres of land, by Judge Plater.

But the last thirty days had taken their toll. John Henry could no longer cry. He had been allowed but one visit a week from his family, and today had been their last. He would be hanged from the old hanging tree in front of the courthouse the next morning to pay for his sin of killing that child.

Justice was swift in Leonardtown. His trial had taken place the week following the tragedy, and his hanging was noted in the newspaper for the first day of July. That was the last day of the court week, and the hanging was sure to draw a nice crowd. John Henry had himself been to several hangings, but this was the first one for a man convicted of killing a child with a carriage, and it was surely the first one in which he would be the star.

***

Grandpa had sent a deckhand to the store to buy him a newspaper, and he brought back the *St. Mary's Beacon*. The story in the paper recounted the facts leading up to the hanging, and after Grandpa read the words, he sat me down and recited them to me, as he thought I was old enough to understand. It was easier to figure out the hanging than it was *A Midsummer's Night Dream.* At least the hanging had a point.

July 1, 1850, was my first hanging, and all the rest of my life—though there were many more such official acts and a few lynchings, too—I would never forget that week. From the bodies floating down the Rappahannock after the hurricane to the drama of the *James Adams Theatre* and the dangling feet of John Henry Plater, life was streaming by in front of me in a quick fashion. When I had first boarded the *Savannah* with my grandfather, I had never planned on seeing all those strange events.

Judge Plater did his best to stop the hanging, but the old judge was too far gone. No one wanted to listen to his pleas for clemency. The retired judge had been off the bench since before Christmas, according to the newspaper that Grandpa had read to Willy and me. The man had made a bold speech on behalf of John Henry, and everyone was amazed that the new judge ignored his predecessor. The newly appointed judge, a contrary fellow by the name of J. Hanson Briscoe, was hell-bent to leather to hang the first man he could in order to get the respect of the voters.

Old Judge Plater had been carried into the courtroom, and when it was time for him to speak, he managed to draw himself up on shaky legs. He took a deep breath, and when he spoke, it was as if he found the voice of God himself. His deep convictions of giving charity and penance to the sinner, instead of consigning him to hell, found no audience with the new judge. After that evening with Grandpa, I made sure to find whatever local newspaper was around to bring back for reading together. By summer's end, I understood a lot of them myself, but they were always more enjoyable when Grandpa read them to me.

I was up early the next morning, and Grandpa allowed me to go with him and Willy to the top of the hill where the large oak tree grew out front of the courthouse. John Henry Plater was brought out from the brick jailhouse nearby, and he walked upon a small platform. A noose was tied around his neck, the other end attached to the hanging tree, and a prayer was said by a minister.

John Henry was allowed last words. He told his family he loved them and was sorry for the mess he had left them. Then the platform was opened, and John Henry's life ended with a twist of rope and snap of bone.

Top: A hanging takes place in a Union Army camp near Petersburg, Va. Bottom: The James Adams Floating Theatre ties up at Leonardtown wharf.

SIX – NOMINI AND A NEW FRIEND

By noon, all those heading to Alexandria and Washington had boarded, and the purser was happy. With a bustling load of passengers and freight, the Savannah would make up the delay thanks to fair weather. The weather was as nice as one could hope for in July. A slight breeze and low humidity marked the first day of what could be a desperately hot month. A wharf jutted out from among several schooners, all rigged for crabbing and fishing. Oyster rakes and tongs were neatly stacked on the shore as the steamboat nudged gently to the dock. Various livestock and freight and a woman with a small girl about my age waited on the wharf next to a large, black travel trunk. Upon laying down the gangplank, the purser greeted the woman and her daughter. He happily welcomed them aboard and offered them the one remaining cabin.

The colored stevedores loaded the luggage and carted it off to her room as the woman, and the child walked around the vessel to inspect their new but temporary home.

As we traveled into Nomini Bay, Grandpa told me that George Washington had grown up on a farm up on the hill. We had learned about the general in school, and Grandpa explained how he had become president. I wondered how farming could prepare a man to be a soldier and President of the United States. I asked Grandpa, and he told me that farmers have to withstand the onslaught of tornados, heat, hurricanes, blizzards, and drought.

"Anyone who can stand up to the elements like that and on Sunday bend on one knee before God and ask for heavenly assistance ought to be able to deal with the varmints and polecats in Washington, D.C.," Grandpa said.

Mostly, I was curious about the girl who had boarded at Nomini Wharf, as she was the only other kid on the ship. By dinner time, the *Savannah* had made it as far as Marshall Hall, where we were going to stop for the night. The time was right for me to speak to the new folks on the *Savannah* because the girl and her mother had joined my table for the evening meal.

"Hello," the young girl said.

"Hello to you," I said, in a burst of bravery.

"Do you live on this boat?" she asked me.

"For the summer, I do."

"Don't you have a home?"

"Yes, but I am a hired hand on this ship, which is the nicest one on the Chesapeake Bay. And my grandfather is the captain."

"Do you get paid?"

"Yep, once a week," I answered. "Now, I have a question for you."

"Yes, what is it?"

"What is your name?"

"Molly Taylor. I'm on my way to the City of Washington with my mother to visit with my father. He works at the War Department, taking care of the big ships and fighting Indians. We are also going to visit my grandfather."

"What does he do?"

"He tells the army when to fight and the Navy when to take trips to far-off places like England and China. Now it's your turn to tell me your name."

"My name is Ethan Aaron Douglas, and I am a champion crab catcher."

***

The next day at breakfast, I asked Molly if she would like a tour of the *Savannah*. After making a trip around the three decks and even down into the freight hold, I guided her to the wheelhouse to meet Willy and Grandpa.

Grandpa let her sit in the captain's chair, and Willy allowed her to steer the ship, giving her a special delight and solidifying myself as a person of importance on the ship, and soon, in her world. We spent the day traveling around the deck and returning to the wheelhouse when the *Savannah* pulled into various wharves as we got closer to Alexandria.

After some passengers left and more arrived at Alexandria, the *Savannah* shoved off for the short trip across the Potomac River to Washington. A railroad bridge had been built to the north of the city dock, and it was quite a sight to see a locomotive hauling a load of passenger and freight cars across the river to Washington, blowing its whistle and bellowing large streams of smoke. I had seen trains before in Georgia, but I had never seen one cross a river.

The dock at Washington was busy with people and boats. Two other steamboats were in port when we pulled in. They were the *Northland* and the *Southland,* both majestic steamships that also worked the Chesapeake Bay. The *Savannah* wasn't as new as those grand steamships, and seeing the differences made me want to ask Grandpa if he had some white paint that I could use to shine the old boat up a bit. There were better things for a kid to do, to be sure, like fishing off the side of the boat or swimming when we tied up at a wharf, but I had taken a liking to the *Savannah*. It had become my home, at least for the summer.

The long line of boats tied up to the Washington wharves came in every size and every type. Fish, crabs, and early season produce were sold right from the boats. Horse-drawn wagons pulled up to take off large loads of fish and freight, and men used wheelbarrows to cart away watermelons and tomatoes. That year had brought an early spring, so by the first week in July, there was a bounty of fresh vegetables for the city folks. People came in droves to shop along the vendor stands that lined the wharves. One of the stands had a big kettle of steaming crabs and a large table piled high with cooked crabs. Baskets filled with the scrambling critters—anxious to get away before being tossed into the kettle—were next to the cooked ones.

Every once in a while, a crab would go scooting across the pier in a desperate dash for the safety of the open water between the dock and the boat. It was the job of one lad about my age to step on it, gingerly reach down and grab the crab from behind, being careful not to let it get him with his sharp pincers, and to toss the blue crab in the kettle to steam. The blue crabs were soon red crabs, and then the fun began.

My grandpa would have me bring him a dozen crabs every evening, or sometimes more, if we stopped for the day. He would proceed to crack open the crabs and wash them down with a large mug of beer. Soon, I found that I had a taste for the crab meat as well, and we would see who could pile up the biggest pile of shells.

While I had been traveling back and forth to Washington for about two months, usually about every two weeks, this was the first time I was sad to leave. My new friend, Molly, had descended from the *Savannah* with her mother to be home in the city for a few weeks with her father and grandfather. But she and her mother would be returning soon, the rest of her family with them, and they would travel back to her mother's home in Cambridge, Maryland. She told me that her mother had already bought tickets for the return trip, and they would once again travel on the *Savannah*. I was looking forward to traveling with Molly.

I figured the voyage down the other side of the bay, after stopping at Baltimore, would take us nearly a week. That trip would give Molly and me plenty of time to catch up on her visit to the City of Washington.

She said they would visit her grandfather, President Zachary Taylor, on the Fourth of July. They were going to a picnic at the White House, then watching fireworks. Molly beamed as she explained life at the White House.

That night, I got Grandpa to tell me what he

knew about the president and the White House. Grandpa told me that Molly's grandfather became president because of his victory in the Mexican War.

I wasn't all that sure what a president did, but I understood the job of a general. I figured that her grandfather wouldn't be a good one to cross and made a note to myself to be on my best behavior when her father came aboard the *Savannah*.

The Three Rivers and the Northland on the Potomac with the U.S. Capitol in the distance.

SEVEN – SLAVES FOR SALE

News at Benedict

When we had arrived in Washington, Molly and her mother were met by a horse-drawn coach. They were the fanciest steeds I had ever seen, and the coach was brilliantly painted.

That night, my grandfather and I also left the ship, something we did only in Washington and

Baltimore, where the steamship company paid for a hotel room for the captain. We were each able to take a hot bath and went to a nice café to eat. Truthfully, we had better food on the *Savannah*, where homemade crab cakes were a daily event, but the hot baths and nice hotel were hard to beat.

The next morning, we walked down to the docks and onto an elevated platform. We stopped to watch the Negroes up for sale at the slave market. Not having had any slaves in our family, the only colored folks I'd had contact with were the stevedores on the *Savannah*, who weren't slaves but free men who worked for wages. Grandpa and I had seen the slave markets in Annapolis and Baltimore, but the one in Washington was held just once a month. Grandpa told me that the sales weren't that good as there wasn't much need in the city for slaves; they were just done for show to prove that they had the legal right to sell and buy slaves in the National City.

Just across the river, in Alexandria, there was a bustling slave trade, and we often passed by the auction house on our way to pick up a newspaper at that port.

We had picked up several newspapers that morning near the hotel, and they would provide plenty for Grandpa and me to read and talk about each evening until we got to Annapolis. We would be able to buy more newspapers there.

Grandpa was reading to me about the slaves and how New Mexico and California were soon to join the Union and not allow slavery. The great debate was all about extending slavery into the soon-to-be new states. Though he owned slaves himself on his plantations in Mississippi and Louisiana, President Taylor made it clear to the Southerners that he would not tolerate talk of secession. He set plans in motion for laws that would allow California and New Mexico to skip the territorial status and create their constitutions immediately, which would ban slavery.

As Grandpa read the articles, he paused and asked me if I had any questions.

"If someone buys a slave and that slave turns out to be faulty, say, he fails to work hard, can they return them for a refund?"

"Boy, that sure sounds reasonable, but the auctioneer states at the beginning of the auction that all sales are final."

"When President Taylor said he would round up and hang anyone who dared to split up the Union, do you think he meant those words?"

"Yes indeed."

***

I didn't realize it at the time, but with our nightly reading of the newspapers, I learned more in my 'summer school' on the *Savannah* than I had back at home in Georgia. What I did know was that I wasn't too anxious to get on the train in Alexandria and head south come October.

When we arrived at Solomon's Island a few days later, having worked all the wharves along the Potomac once again, we heard the terrible news; the President had taken deathly ill on the Fourth of July and was near death.

Mrs. Langley, our cook, had kin on Solomon's Island, and when our ship came into the dock, her relatives were waiting to greet her.

After leaving Solomon's Island, the mighty *Savannah* lumbered north up the Patuxent River, stopping at more than a dozen wharves, and each of them contributed more to our holds of freight and livestock. Our last stop was Benedict, where, Grandpa explained, a British fleet had unloaded an army that marched on Washington in 1814, burning the White House and the Capitol, then sailing back downriver to the Chesapeake to attack Baltimore. My imagination filled in all the pauses between Grandpa reading the newspaper. But I couldn't imagine the words he read in Benedict.

The president had died. I feared not for the country but whether Molly would board the *Savannah* as planned in a couple of weeks. What I didn't know until the following summer was that she and her family had taken a train to Kentucky, where they buried her grandfather. President Taylor had taken sick of cholera on the Fourth of July and died five days later. I was sorry for him and Molly, but I was mostly sorry to have missed the joy of having Molly on my boat once more.

"Vice President Millard Fillmore was sworn in as President," Grandpa read. "They came up with a compromise on slavery, and California and New

Mexico are petitioning for statehood. There's going to be more stars to go with the bars on the flag, lad."

EIGHT - SHORE MAYHEM

The remainder of that voyage to Annapolis and Baltimore, then down the Eastern Shore of Maryland, was very different from the first leg. A hurricane, a hanging, meeting Molly—my first and only girlfriend—and a dead president had all taken place during one trip on the Savannah.

How anything more exciting could ever take place,

I wondered. Part of the job of a steamboat was also to carry the news port to port. Now that I was becoming a regular newsreader, I began to help spread the news. Not too many folks cared to learn their news from 'a young whippersnapper,' as the old folks would say, but a few folks would listen, and I did my best to keep it all straight.

When we arrived at Cambridge, which was two days out of Baltimore, we heard about the great compromise on slavery; we soon ran into the reality. Part of the compromise had been to enact new laws regarding fugitive slaves. At Cambridge, there was a trial ready to start for a Lutheran minister charged with helping more than a dozen slaves escape from a plantation near the town. The minister was facing a significant fine and jail time if he was convicted.

The newspaper said he was part of the Underground Railroad. Grandpa said it wasn't a railroad at all but a group of cellars, barns, and smokehouses for escaped slaves to hide in during the day before traveling north at night. Grandpa said that at the rate they were going, the colored folks would all live in cities instead of working on farms. Because we had been able to attend the hanging in Leonardtown, I asked Grandpa if we could stop in Cambridge overnight to be there for the minister's trial.

"Ethan, that trial could last a week," Grandpa said. "There is a big-time lawyer from Baltimore down for this great event, and the merchants will all want the judge to string it out, so the bars, restaurants, and hotels all do a good business. People even came in from Philadelphia and Washington by boat and train. Plenty of northerners who oppose slavery are here, too. It's going to last a long time, and we can read about the latest when we get back in two weeks."

Our trip down the Eastern Shore of Maryland took us into lots of wharves at farms and plantations. We also stopped at villages like St. Michaels, Oxford, and Crisfield. Tangier Island in Virginia, and Smith Island, in Maryland, were our regular stops along with landings in more plantations on the Virginia Eastern Shore. Then it was back to Norfolk, where the busy port barely noticed a single ship like ours. There were more than a dozen steamboats at the terminal in Norfolk when we arrived. Several Navy ships, including a new steam and sail warship, passed by us as the *Savannah* continued on its way into the harbor.

My news reading had been gaining attention from the passengers, many of whom could not read. Thus Grandpa suggested I might read for a group of passengers in the saloon while the *Savannah* was underway.

I was a bit nervous about my new duty, but Mrs. Langley told me she would whip up my favorite crab soup to hear me read, so it was a good deal. She arrived in the saloon the first day I gave a read, and I was promptly rewarded with a steaming bowl of her scrumptious crab soup, which was made with tomatoes.

The passengers took a liking to me reading the newspaper stories to them, and some asked me to read the ads as well. Then someone asked me to read the obituaries. After I finished, a few of the passengers walked by and gave me a penny, some as much as a nickel!

Some days I made as much as twenty-five cents, all for doing what I was going to do anyway. The newspapers usually only cost me a penny. That was some rich living for a country boy!

Grandpa said I needed to save what I was making and invest my money. When we returned to Washington, he took me to a bank and had me open an account.

By the end of the summer, I had saved more than twenty dollars. When it was time to return to Georgia for the school year, he gave me an extra twenty dollars to add to my savings. He also paid for my train ticket south and gave me ten dollars to cover any meals and to get me started in school. In addition to my newfound wealth, I had gained an ability to not only read adult writing but also to recite them to an audience. I would keep this a secret from my teacher, as I could see nothing good coming from it—just more schoolwork.

Before the summer was over, we had returned to Cambridge several times, and I was anxious to read about the minister's trial. He had been convicted of the high crime of aiding fugitive slaves. Because he was a local minister, the judge sentenced him to aid the poor and suspended the one-year jail sentence and the fine. The sentence could have been reinstated if the minister continued to aid fugitive slaves. The two slaves who had been caught in his cellar were returned to the plantation they had fled. When I read that news story to the passengers on the *Savannah*, there were many discussions afterward, with many opposed to slavery and others furious that the minister had received such easy treatment. Grandpa later told me that the division among the passengers reflected the nation, and it worried him. With President Taylor gone, Grandpa said that President Fillmore wasn't doing anything to keep the country together as talk of secession grew.

NINE - A NEW JOB

It was spring again, and when I got off the train in Alexandria, Virginia, Grandpa, Willy, and Mrs. Langley were all at the station to meet me.

"Well, lad, looks like you have grown a couple of inches, and you could use some larger shirts."

"Grandpa, I have some more clothes in my bag. I didn't want to get them dirty traveling on the train. You have to have the windows open, but then the cinders and ash come in. Traveling on a steamboat is a lot better, fresh air and all."

"Perhaps we can have you write the ads for the company," Grandpa said with a laugh.

As we walked from the train station and boarded the *Savannah*, Grandpa told me that I had a new job, that of newsreader and entertainer. It paid more money; I would get the grand pay of one dollar a day. Of course, I would have to keep up with my other chores as deckhand of the wheelhouse.

"One of the passengers last fall was from the company, and he was with us from Baltimore to Norfolk," Grandpa said. "He enjoyed your talks and reading so much, and he saw how the passengers took to your routine that he decided you get a raise. They are going to find teachers who are out of school for the summer to do the same thing on the other company steamboats. It looks like you started a trend."

Before we made it to Annapolis, I had not only read the newspapers to the folks in the saloon each day, but I had even dug out some of that Shakespeare fella's writings and began to read them, performing all of the characters myself. With folks laughing and carrying on, the time passed quickly, and I received lots of tips in addition to my regular pay. I wondered if I could get a job at that *James Adams Floating Theatre*. Maybe Molly would be on board one day and hear me recite *Romeo and Juliet*. That would be something.

I didn't have to wait for an imaginary job in order to see Molly again. She and her mother boarded the next day, once more in Nomini Bay, Virginia, where they visited relatives. Her father still worked in the War Department even though her grandfather had died. When she came aboard, I thought my heart would leap out of my chest. I was convinced that we would grow up, get married, and live the rest of our lives together. I hadn't figured out the part of being a newsreader on a steamboat and how that would support a family, but then, I was only eleven and had plenty of time to figure it all out.

That first afternoon, during the appointed time for me to read—one o'clock until about four o'clock—Molly had a front-row seat. She was excited to learn about my promotion. She was a pretty girl, with long braided hair and wearing a bright yellow sundress that lit up the room. Her smile was that of an angel, and she had the cutest little dimples in each cheek. Her blue eyes and her look of devotion as she hung on my every word made me believe that my expectations and dreams might come true. I started off a little rusty because I was a bit nervous, but soon I was crooning and swooning, the crowd delighting in my delivery of the news and *A Midsummer's Night Dream*. In short, I had become a ham and loved playing the part; the crowd loved it as well. I could imagine not just the floating theatre but the stage of the big National Theatre we drove by in Washington.

The summer went by quickly, and I was amazed that Molly had talked her mother into reasons to visit relatives in Virginia and her father in Washington at least every other week. Her mother's parents were wealthy planters in Maryland, and President Taylor had left his plantations in the south to her father to supervise. Therefore, Molly and her mother were able to travel without worrying about the cost. I was just glad that they hadn't opted to take the more luxurious steamboats.

The *Savannah* was nearly as large as any steamboat on the Chesapeake Bay. The hold could carry lots of freight and helped the ship keep its balance to counter the three decks above. The main deck was carrying wagon loads of cargo, livestock, and fresh produce. The forward deck was open, and often there were loads of timber stacked on it. The aft end was where the passengers' staterooms were located. There were twenty-five cabins with room for two passengers in each. The center of the first deck went up two levels with a grand saloon filled with chairs and a piano. Day passengers would congregate there as well as on the open decks. The ship could carry as many as four hundred for excursions from Washington to Marshall Hall.

Whenever a passenger who could play the old walnut piano came aboard, I was eager to get lessons. It was my good luck that Molly had been taking lessons and, when she was traveling with us, she would teach me. There were more staterooms on the top level, but they were costly. There were six of them, and Molly and her mother stayed in one of them when they traveled on the *Savannah*.

The very best accommodations on the ship were those provided for the captain. Therefore, we had the best view of anyone, but it was the farthest distance to the galley. There were always upsides and downsides, as Grandpa would say.

The chief advantage that any ship had was its captain, and Captain Douglas, as others called him, was among the best on the bay. He knew when to make the long run around Point Lookout to the Patuxent River and when to pull into a safe harbor at St. Mary's City or Wynne, along the Maryland shore of the Potomac. When a gale blew up, the timetable blew up too, as Grandpa said. It was a desirable schedule, weather permitting.

The ship had loaded a full bunker of coal in Washington, where it docked at the Seventh Street Wharf. A coal train came right into the wharves to load the ships every day. The coal kept the boilers going, which in turn provided the steam to turn the driveshaft, which powered the large stern wheel. The new ships had two wheels—one on each side—which offered more maneuverability, but a good helmsman like Willy could gently move the 175-foot ship into just about any place he wanted.

Some of the wharves, like those at Kinsale, Virginia, or Bromes Wharf at St. Mary's City, were located on calm creeks; others, such as Aquia Creek on the Virginia shore or Newburg on the Maryland side, were more open. If the wind was blowing, docking could be treacherous.

While I entertained the passengers in the afternoon in the salon, the gamblers ran their poker games in a smoking parlor near the aft deck. I wasn't allowed in the smoking parlor, and from the looks of some of the gamblers on that riverboat, I didn't want to be near them anyway.

By the time of my fifth summer on the *Savannah*, my mother had decided to move up to Virginia. We had relatives near Washington, so that I would be living near my Grandpa and my family. My sisters and three brothers were all getting older, and the oldest brother—who had turned eleven—joined me on the *Savannah*. He got my old job as a cabin boy and all-around helper. William was a big kid and was soon able actually to be a help instead of a tagalong. I was having a great time on the *Savannah* as the official news-reader and entertainer, and I had injected poetry and magic tricks into my routine. Molly asked if she could work on the *Savannah*, too, but her mother firmly quashed that idea. Still, she and her mother managed to travel on the steamboat at least once a month, and because I was out of school and working year-round on the ship, I saw her quite often. Her mother's hovering presence grew stronger as we grew older.

I knew from my grandfather that the rancor

over the issue of slavery was going to lead the southern states to secede from the Union. He told me that there didn't seem to be any leaders who would be able to keep that awful fate from happening to the nation we all loved.

Those who owned slaves, for the most part, wanted to keep them. Those who were slaves, overwhelmingly, wanted their freedom. Many in the north had made money bringing slaves to the south, having bought them from African chiefs or European traders and selling them for a hefty profit. The northern economy was reliant on cheap labor from immigrants—itself a form of slave labor—but many northerners had a strong resentment of slavery. For the most part, I found it better to skip most of the news about slavery and instead read to the passengers about the increasing immigration of Europeans to America and the gold rush in California. Many from the east were heading west for new lands and new opportunities, even while the east was booming.

Each time I read about the gold rush in the west and learned more about the wars over the "white gold," or oysters, on the Chesapeake Bay, I yearned to be more than an entertainer.

Because William was a bit of a ham himself, I coached him on reading and soon had him reading the news to the passengers. We would spend an hour each day selecting books and reading them in the small library. All of William's first summer was spent preparing him to replace me. Grandpa knew what we were doing, and he chuckled, saying he would soon have his entertainment times doubled. The only path for me to move on past this wonderful time in my life was to have William take over. Soon, he was able to do so, and I was free to pursue a new opportunity. I made my move. When we were in port at Cobb Island, I heard from a mate on an oyster buyboat that his captain was looking for a deckhand.

***

Captain James Cullison was sitting on his big chair in the wheelhouse of his large buyboat, the *Maryland Lady*. Cullison and his crew sailed the Potomac, the Patuxent, and the Chesapeake Bay, buying oysters from the watermen. The watermen were able to use their time tonging the oysters and pulling them up from the rich oyster bars located on the bay's bottom and the rivers. Captain Cullison had a fleet of buyboats that worked the rivers and the bay, and he had amassed a fortune. He lived in a large manor home overlooking the Wicomico River near Cobb Island, where one of his buyboats was docked, while ten others were set up in similar operations around the Chesapeake. With his oyster money, he had been one of the original investors in the Baltimore and Ohio Railroad, as well as the Pennsylvania Railroad. He was a wise man who saw the future and had invested in the Norfolk and Western railroad as well. He gave me a job working as a deckhand, but I had learned from my previous job to keep up with the news, and at every chance, I read any newspaper I could get my hands on. By that time, President James Buchanan had taken over in the White House, and in the view of Captain Cullison, secession was near.

Cargo ships in port at Alexandria, Virginia

TEN - MARRYING MOLLY

Working a buyboat was only somewhat easier than pulling the oysters up off the bottom of the rivers and bay. The next most challenging line of work on the water to that of tonging oysters was to be a deckhand on a buyboat. Not long into my new job, I realized what a gem of a job I had given to my brother William.

Buyboats worked the entire year, but it was

September through April that the oysters were seriously harvested. The need to keep them cold on the way to market required the oysters to be on ice. Ice was rare; thus, tradition held that any month with an "R" in it was a suitable time to harvest oysters.

Oysters were in high demand, and the supply was endless. Our buyboat would fill its hold with oysters from the oystermen and return to Washington and Baltimore to sell them to the wholesalers. They were shucked and sent in ice to major cities by train. They were then sold by the dozens of bushels to markets and hotels. Sometimes we would make the trip down to Norfolk, our hold bursting with oysters when prices weren't what Captain Cullison thought was fair.

The other part of my lament over giving up my easy—although low-paying—job to my brother William was that I would rarely see Molly. She was a great letter writer, and I became one, too. Grandpa had advised me to use my mother's address in Virginia.

I made a trip about once every other month to see my mother and family and to pick up my letters from Molly. When my buyboat went to Washington, the captain usually stayed for a day, which allowed me to catch the train from Alexandria to my mother's home in Leesburg on the Washington and Old Dominion Line. I would travel out on the slow train the forty-five miles to Leesburg, spend the night, and travel back the next day. If the *Mary-*

land Lady left without me, I would be docked my pay and had to catch up with it by hitching a ride on the next steamboat heading downriver.

I really didn't care if I missed the *Maryland Lady* because my pay was pretty good, and I was sometimes able to meet the *Savannah* and visit with William and my grandfather. I was also able to read each letter from Molly about ten times.

The *Maryland Lady* was the pride of Captain Cullison's fleet. It had been constructed at Deltaville, Virginia, at a large shipyard. I soon knew every inch of the ship, which operated on both sail and steam power. After working for the captain for five years, fate got me a promotion.

The captain assigned to work the *Maryland Lady* for Captain Cullison ran off to Virginia when the War Between the States began, and Captain Cullison called me into his office at Cobb Island.

"Son, you have done a good job. Old Captain Douglas trained you well, though I was certainly skeptical that a young man who had such a solid reputation as an entertainer would make a good deckhand," Captain Cullison said. "But you have proven your worth. Because Captain Johnny became Johnny Reb, you are now Captain Ethan Douglas, the master of the *Maryland Lady.* This new job will require, of course, that you no longer miss a day by going off to Leesburg."

"I don't think that is a problem, sir. The Yankees have been making it hard to run that train out to the Shenandoah Valley, and when they aren't stopping it to check for rebels, the rebels are raiding it to get supplies. I don't know how the railroad can stay in business with this war raging."

One detail I ironed out was to affirm that I, as master of my vessel, could allow a visitor. I included the news in what turned out to be my last letter to Molly, sent via my mother in Leesburg. I asked Molly to meet me in Baltimore so she could travel south on the bay with me, where I would take her home to Cambridge. When I arrived on the *Maryland Lady* at the large freight terminal in Baltimore, Molly was standing in the October sun with a bright yellow sundress and jacket to shield her from the dropping fall temperatures. I hoped she had warmer clothes for our trip south. Her mother had accompanied her by train and ferry to Baltimore from the Eastern Shore. She intended to chaperone us, as well as to shop in the big city.

The *Maryland Lady* was on an overnight trip in Baltimore, so I took a room at a modest hotel—very different from Molly's accommodations at the Lord Baltimore Hotel in the downtown area. The streets were alive with rebel talk, and a large riot had been put down by Yankee troops the week before we arrived. The Republican Lincoln had been elected, and the first states had seceded from the Union. They said that when Lincoln traveled to Washington from Illinois, he had to virtually go without any fanfare because of fears about his safety in Baltimore.

While the talk of war turned into acts of war,

my thoughts were of chasing the white gold that had given me a very comfortable salary and, of course, of Molly. Captain Cullison had shown me how to use my savings to buy stock in his railroads, and all three companies were doing well. Molly's mother allowed us to go to dinner without her, as she was to dine with old friends.

It was that night, after walking around the city following dinner, that I proposed to my one and only love, and she accepted.

"I have one question for you, Ethan."

"What is that?"

"What in the world took you so long? I have had my bags packed for a year."

As I could travel easily, I had Molly pick us out a nice house in her family's hometown. We were married at Christmas, barely giving her time to get together a wedding befitting the granddaughter of a president and the daughter of a U. S. Congressman.

The wreck of the steamer Mary Washington.

USS Fort Donnellson (former blockade runner Robert E. Lee).

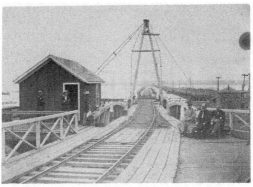

Railroad bridge over the Potomac River at Washington, D.C.

ELEVEN - WAR ON THE CHESAPEAKE AND POTOMAC

At first, the War Between the States didn't affect us much on the water. We had been having our own war for quite a while. The

Eastern Shore watermen would battle those from the Western Shore; the Maryland watermen would battle those from Virginia.

The mouth of the Chesapeake Bay was in Confederate-held territory. At the same time, the middle and upper bay areas were dominated by those who were either sympathetic to the South or whose sons had already left and joined the Confederate Army or Navy. These areas were also under the military control of the Union forces.

My grandfather was disgusted with both sides' politicians in Washington and having two governments made for that many more opportunities for hapless politicians of little talent to bluster and bully.

That was Grandpa's view, and Captain Cullison was of the same mind. They were the two smartest men I knew, so following their lead on the matter worked for me. I would stay with my boat, but I was worried about William. He was getting to be a big kid, and the adventure promised by joining the Confederate army had his mind whirling. I had seen enough of the bloodshed in the various engagements of the Oyster Wars on the Potomac to know it was senseless and not for me.

The federal ships were plentiful, and more were being built, some of them right on the Eastern Shore and in Baltimore. There was a shipyard on Solomon's Island building sloops, which the Union Navy was taking as fast as they could be built. The Union Navy was serious about being able to control the Potomac River and the Chesapeake Bay. The Union was out to cut off the Confederate ports from trade with Europe and the Caribbean.

***

While I worked hard to show Captain Cullison he had made the right decision in promoting me to captain of the *Maryland Lady*, my brother William kept up the news reading on the *Savannah*.

Blockades and picket ships were everywhere on the east coast and up into the reaches of the Chesapeake and its tributaries. The following was an update on the war from the *New York Times*, read by William:

> In dispatches from Havana show that commerce by steam and sailing vessels is regular between that port and the ports of southern states and more frequent than with the blockade. It is reported that Confederate ministers, Messrs. Slidell and Johnson, did go from Charleston to Cuba in a Confederate steamer, but not the Nashville, as reported.

***

As much as the federal Navy was out to stop the flow of shipping to southern ports, the fledgling new nation was quickly taking steps to maintain its flow of commerce with overseas ports. In addition, the Confederacy was also busily connecting with foreign powers. Britain was especially interested in doing anything possible to see its former colonies split apart, and they continued to trade with the South. My old job as a newsreader on the steamboat had prepared me well for my job as master of the *Maryland Lady*. Captain Cullison told me that I had gained many advantages of a college education by reading and reciting. Grandpa agreed and said that somewhere along the line, one couldn't help but profit from all that reading.

I was soon of the mind that I needed to run my boat, make sure I kept expenses in check, and get my loads to market.

While all the ballyhoo was going on and folks were off to fight and kill their own kinfolk, I decided to stay out of the war.

Captain Cullison's fortunes were divided by his significant stock ownership of two railroads that operated primarily in the north and the other that operated in the south. He decided to keep his fleet of buyboats in operation because seafood was as essential a part of American diets as chickens and beef.

With such an attitude, that meant we caught hell from both sides. The Yankees were always stopping our boats and inspecting them for spies, and each time would cart off a dozen bushels of oysters. The Rebs would board us at gunpoint, looking for Yankee spies, and they would also take a dozen bushels with them. Make no mistake, we were heavily armed, but those weapons were to protect us from the typical oyster warfare. We did not fire on military vessels. There was no future in doing so, Captain Cullison said.

War was just as difficult for the three major steamboat companies that worked the bay. Because they hauled a considerable deal of the freight between the three major cities and all of the small towns, farms, and plantations along the bay and its tributaries, they had to continue to operate. Just a few months after the war began, the Union decided to blockade the ports of the south. That meant Norfolk and Hampton Roads were closed to shipping, including steamboats until the Union Navy took control of those areas.

Grandpa was over seventy, but his health was still good. He said he could go live with my mother or go back to his home in Georgia, but either way, the war was close to both places. At least if he kept his position on the *Savannah*, he could keep a solid and firm hand on William. At that point, William was fifteen, and my younger brother John worked as the cabin boy for Grandpa. With the war on, working on the *Savannah* seemed to be plenty of adventure for both of them, and Grandpa kept them on a tight rein.

A Yankee detachment was sent on the *Savannah* when she went south to Norfolk and returned up the Potomac. That meant there were six freeloaders who expected to eat for free and spent their time loafing. The *Savannah* didn't usually have soldiers on board for the trip to Baltimore, but leaving that city for Norfolk, they joined the ship.

On one trip up the Potomac, when passing Coles Point at about midnight, a small sloop silently pulled alongside the *Savannah* without drawing any notice from those on board and slipped a woman onto the ship. The sloop disappeared into the dark night. The Yankee soldiers were fast asleep, having had too much beer with their hard crabs. The woman blended in with the other passengers in the saloon and the next morning left the ship at the 7th Street Wharf in Washington. On other occasions, she boarded with other passengers at various stops. About once a month, she simply climbed aboard when the *Savannah* neared Coles Point. Of course, her presence was known to Grandpa and the crew, but they put transporting a Confederate spy in the same category as giving free rides to Union troops. It was something they would have to put up with until the end of the war.

***

William read of events of the day to the passengers.

From the Alexandria Gazette:

"Virginia was determined by the act of the Richmond Convention passing a secession ordinance. By that act, all persons in the State became rebels—Hence in reorganizing a new government, it was proper that those who did not wish to be included in the rebellion should take or retake the oath of allegiance. Therefore the act of the Convention was eminently proper, and all officials of every character should be compelled to take the oath of allegiance or surrender their positions. In law, no notice of a requisition to take the oath was necessary, but this Court was one of equity and would not undertake to oust officers, who had not had notice of the oath required of them."

"What they are trying to say, folks is that you

became a rebel, like it or not, due to what the Richmond Convention did. If you consider yourself not in rebellion and live in Virginia, you have to retake the oath of allegiance or surrender your elected office," William explained.

"Also from the *Alexandria Gazette* are the following items of interest for your perusal and consideration here on the *Savannah*."

"We learn that the Mansion House Hotel of this city will shortly be occupied by the forces of the United States as a Military Hospital. The Hotel is the most commodious and one of the most splendid buildings in this city."

"A petition to the Secretary of War has been sent by "loyal citizens of the United States, resident in Washington and Georgetown," asking him to take steps to prevent the extortion now practiced in the sale of wood and coal—induced by, as they allege, a combination and monopoly such as existed uniting the flour dealers in April last. They denounce the present prices of fuel as unnecessary the attempt thus made to harass, oppress, and ruin the citizens, and ask for protection."

William kept the flow of information going.

"The captain of the schooner Susquehanna, (a colored man) which sailed from Alexandria, on the 15th for Philadelphia, has arrived at the latter port and furnishes an account of his running the Potomac blockade."

'When passing south on the Potomac at Quantico, the balls from the batteries there going entirely across the river but escaped without having his vessel struck. He could see neither guns nor fortifications, but the cannonballs were unmistakable."

***

My grandfather warned me of some of the romance of going off to fight that began to sink in my brother William's mind as he read more reports of casualties to the passengers. The Alexandria Gazette carried a report from Missouri:

"The Pilot Knob (Missouri,) correspondent of the St. Louis Democrat, speaking of the late battle at Fredericktown in that State says, that '" a greater portion of the dead and wounded were boys from fifteen to eighteen years old, mere striplings, with the down on their faces.'"

Capt. Jervis, a Member of Parliament, has made a speech at a Conservative meeting in favor of the right of Secession and urging the people of England to give as strong an expression of their sentiments as would induce the Government to act accordingly.

The Baltimore American of today says:

"Scouts have brought in word that Gen. George Johnston occupies Martinsburg with five regiments and that stirring times are expected by the Federal pickets of the Twelfth Indiana Regiment stationed in that vicinity."

"The Comanche's and Utah's have been locking horns near Maxwell's Ranch, originating from a theft committed by the Utah's, in which they obtained 100 head of Comanche horses. The Comanche's followed to them and gunfight ensued and in the struggle, many of their number were killed."

"A dispatch from San Francisco reports a terrible gale having occurred at Mazatlan, blowing down houses and wrecking ships at a fearful rate."

Thomas F. Goode, a well-known politician and is now a private in the 2d regiment Virginia Cavalry, wants to represent the Fifth District in that State in the next Congress. The election for President and Vice President takes place in the new Confederacy next week.

The Southern people are quite indignant at the fact of the Comte de Paris having volunteered in the United States Army. A correspondent of the Charleston Courier hopes that one of their sharpshooters will pick off the young sprig of royalty.

They are making preparations to run ambulances on the railroad trains between Manassas and Richmond.
The United States Marshal at Wheeling has seized the property of Charles W. Russell, Esq., in that city, as subject to confiscation, the owner being in the Confederate army. Mr. Russell is now an aide to Gen. Lee, was a lawyer of considerable prominence, and, at the time of his departure from Wheeling, was counsel for the Baltimore and Ohio Railroad in a case of much importance.

The retirement of Lieutenant General Scott raises Major General McClellan to the position of commander-in-chief of the armies of the United States unless the President should veto it, which is scarcely probable, or to appoint no one else to that position. After the death of Major General Macomb, Gen. (Scott followed his successor, over the head of Admiral Games, his senior officer, to the great displeasure of the latter. Since the battle of Ball's Bluff, a great deal of the friends of the wounded soldiers visited the hospitals at Poolesville. The Washington correspondent of the Philadelphia Enquirer says: "Several hundred people from Massachusetts and Pennsylvania come on to see their wounded relatives' friends at Poolesville. They are rowing out daily."

The Baltimore American (Union) pronounces a recent article in the National Intelligencer (Union) in regard to Maryland, "highly injudicious."

The families of Clay and Chittenden in Kentucky are all divided by the present civil war—some of each belonging to the opposing sides.

Col. Henry L. Scott, one of the Inspectors
General, and son-in-law of Lieut. Gen. Scott has been retired by the army board owing to his physical disability.

Rev. Dr. Butler of Washington goes to Cincinnati to a church in the latter city.

A letter from an officer on board the Federal steamer Pawnee, off Old Point, to the Philadelphia Press, states that the iron-clad Confederate steamer Merrimac has shown herself several times recently. She steams down the Elizabeth River from Norfolk and generally lays in the vicinity.

The Federal prisoners of this State being confined in Fort Lafayette were on Wednesday removed to Fort Warren, in Boston harbor. Among the number are thirty-six citizens of Maryland, principally from Baltimore. The object of their removal is not stated.

Major Eaton's purchases of subsistence at New York the first quarter of the present year amounted to $100,000. His purchases for the second quarter amounted to $750,000. For the third, ending October 1st, the amount has been largely increased.

General Shields was at Matalan on the 13th of October. He declines the appointment of Brigadier General. He is encouraging some land for Irish emigrants to settle in the Western States of Mexico.

The Washington correspondent of the Baltimore Sun says, that letters from Republicans in the West, affirm that Adjutant General Thomas has actually understated matters in reference to Gen. Fremont.

The steamer Arago, from Southampton on the 10th ultimo, has arrived in New York, bringing a complete supply of army equipment and clothing for twelve thousand men.

At about ten o'clock on Wednesday morning, a boat, with what was supposed to be a flag of truce, was seen coming across the Potomac from the mouth of Quantico Creek. Captain Adams of the First Massachusetts Regiment went down to the shore at Budd's Ferry to receive it. When within about a thousand yards from the Maryland side, the men in the boat threw overboard a barrel, which they anchored like a buoy. Taking in the flag, they sailed back to the Virginia side as fast as possible. After reaching land, the same flag was flaunted by one of the crew over the battery at Shipping Point.

In the afternoon, heavy firing was heard down the Potomac from Budd's Ferry.

The Spanish fleet for the invasion of Mexico leaves Havana as soon as the squadron arrives from Spain —in all, 12 steam vessels of war and 300 guns. Unless the demands of Spain are met in the right spirit, with good promises to fill their obligations and comply with the Miramon treaty, the fleet will take the best security it can obtain, and by force if necessary, calculating to be sustained by France and England.

The citizens of Buffalo, claiming General Heintzelman as a townsman, have petitioned the President to appoint him Major-General.

The list of signers begins with former President Millard Fillmore.

The King of Prussia was crowned with great pomp

and splendor at Konigsberg on the 18th of last month. At the conclusion of the ceremony, his Majesty delivered a very impressive and animated address.

The Navy Department has just ordered 500 more rifled cannon, and immense quantities of shot and shell are in the course of preparation.

Col. Wm. B. Mann of Pennsylvania has resigned his commission in the Federal army.

***

So went an afternoon's worth of information for the passengers of the *Savannah* as William became more and more capable in his job as a newsreader.

***

The *Maryland Lady* crew worked hard and made lots of money for Captain Cullison and a good salary for me. One morning at about five o'clock, the Maryland Lady slipped her moorings at Cobb Island to make her rounds among the watermen. It was nearly winter, the first of the war. When reaching the Virginia side of St. Clement's Island, we neared a sloop over the top of a productive oyster bar.

Shots rang out as we sailed nearby, and a smaller craft appeared from behind the sloop. Men on both boats aimed deadly fire at each other, and I watched as two men were hit by gunfire and slumped to their decks. The gunfire seemed to rage forever before it finally ceased. Either they ran out of bullets, or they were all dead. After waiting for about fifteen minutes to make sure they were through shooting at each other, as choosing sides in that battle could be deadly, we slowly made our way alongside the large oyster sloop.

The smaller vessel, about twenty-one feet in length, was drifting about thirty feet from the larger one. Three bodies lay slumped on the deck of the small boat, and we could see four dead bodies lying in various locations on the larger one.

After hailing the sloop Mabel Ann several times and getting no answer, one of our deckhands hopped aboard after we edged carefully over to her. Someone must have fired the last shot, but no one seemed to be alive.

As our deckhand moved down into the hatch to inspect the hold, another shot rang out, and Robert, our deckhand, quickly came back up the ladder and fired his gun down into the area as he retreated. The hold was nearly full of oysters, and the bottom was thick, so there wasn't much chance of Robert shooting a hole in the hull, and it was clear to us; he wasn't trying to hit an oyster. There was, or at least there had been, someone left alive.

"Come up out of there. We aren't here to hurt you. Toss that pistol out first," Robert said.

A young boy of about fifteen threw out his gun and came up the ladder. Robert brought him aboard the *Maryland Lady* while our deckhands secured a tow line to the *Mabel Ann*, which was a boat from Piney Point, Maryland. The small boat had no markings on it and was likely either a pirate vessel or simply out to capture a prize for the Confederates. Whichever was the case, we weren't about to tow it back to Virginia—not during a war — so it remained adrift. Either the Confederates or the vultures would find the boat as the tide carried it to the Virginia shore.

It took us about an hour to reach Piney Point, and we ran up St. George Creek 'til we arrived at where the lad said his father's dock was located. George Goddard, his father, and three other men lay dead after having been ambushed. That day had been the deadliest in the Oyster Wars. Young Tom Goddard had just become the youngest captain in that area. He was the oldest son and would need to continue working the water to support his mother and three sisters. We helped young Tom unload the bodies of his father and his crew, then we bought his load of oysters and transferred the catch into our hold.

The Yankees were building a prison camp and hospital down at Point Lookout, and lots of ships were bringing in supplies. A federal Navy ship hailed us as we left St. George Creek and entered the Potomac, so we slowed to meet her.

"Hello, Captain, we need to arrange to buy some oysters from you," a young Union lieutenant said, standing on the bow of the patrol vessel.

"We have a market for these oysters already, sir."

"Now you have a new one. Here are my orders, and this purchase invoice will show you how to obtain payment from the government."

"Does that mean you are simply stealing our oysters?"

"No, Captain, the government will pay you a fair price for your oysters. We will follow you down to Point Lookout, where you can deliver the load."

As we headed south down the Potomac to deliver about two hundred bushels of oysters to the army camp, I figured we were working in the middle of two wars. Life had changed on the Chesapeake, to be sure.

***

There must be a decidedly lively time down the Potomac, especially at Budd's Ferry, on the Maryland shore, and at Quantico and about there on the Virginia shore. Mr. Posey and his family living near Budd's Ferry are under arrest. The Federal troops are putting up batteries and are very active in finding out those who are suspected of giving information to the Confederates across the river. They are in pursuit of a Mr. Lemuel Hannon, charged with this offense.

The determination to make promotions in the United States Army from deserving men in the ranks is said to be received with great pleasure by the soldiers and to give much satisfaction to all. We have never doubted the excellence of the system in the army—nor do we believe that the extension of plan to the navies of great powers will hinder their efficiency.

The New York Times publishes a letter from a correspondent in Washington, dated 4 October 28, in which the writer says: "Of course there are a thousand conjectures as to the destination of the great naval expedition, but I rather suspect its field of operations will be along Pamlico Sound."

Gen. McClellan if so much incommoded by visitors of curiosity, that he has had "self-defense, to exclude visitors, except on very important business. It is said in the Washington Star that Col. Ashford of Fairfax County is now dead; we have but not confirmed, in perfect and contradictory accounts of skirmishes and war.

The Court then took up the case of Sergeant Coglan of the 'Lincoln Cavalry".

Charged with shooting at Mr. John Kerr. Messrs. Quinsby, John L. Smith, John Kerr, and A. J. Walker were examined as witnesses in the case.
It appeared in evidence that the accused was in the Shoe Store of John L. Smith, Saturday night last, somewhat intoxicated that after ordering a pair of boots, he approached Mr. John Kerr, who was sitting the store, and asked 'Are there many secessionists in this town ?" to which Kerr replied that "he believed there were a few, "when the accused took out his pistol, and further asked 'Are you a secessionist?" to which Kerr replied that "he was an old man and did not take part." The accused then turned to Walker, who had just come in, and inquired, "What are you?" Walker answered, "l am a Shoemaker" As the accused turned to Walker, Kerr started to pass into the residence of Mr. Smith by a back door. The accused, seeing Kerr move, cocked his pistol and called to him to halt. Kerr did not halt, and as he passed the door, the accused fired his pistol,

the ball passing through the partition above Kerr's head.

A guard was then called, and the accused arrested. The accused soldier said he had been drinking and was unconscious of the action that he had never been in Alexandria before. Still, he supposed that while in delirium, produced by drink, he had been thinking of injuries done him whilst a resident of Georgia and of the talk of the soldiers in regard to Alexandria being a secession place, and this led him, unconsciously to commit the deed.

The Court said that no man, soldier or otherwise, had a right to ask anybody their sentiments and that it intended to protect all peaceable people in carrying on their business, but as it was evident there was no personal malice, in this case, he would postpone its further consideration until tomorrow, to give time for the accused to present witness as to his character.

On the way back to port, we bought the catch of six other sloops, none of which had been near or knew about the slaughter on the river near St. Clements Island. We pulled in at Cobb Island, where I gave the Army paperwork to Captain Cullison.

"We will never see any money from this robbery," he said. "But carry it on to Washington with you anyway, and take the invoice to the address shown on their order. You have to take your load there anyway, so we might as well find out if they will really pay the bill."

To Captain Cullison's great surprise, the Army paid for the invoice and many more after that, quickly becoming one of our best customers. They were willing to pay a premium for shucked oysters, so Captain Cullison set up a shucking house on Smith Creek, not far from Point Lookout. He also started a tomato factory, canning and shipping tomatoes. The Army was the prime customer for those too. Captain Cullison began to make a lot of money off the Union, which needed supplies for its camp and the vast numbers of troops based in Washington. In Virginia, the Norfolk and Western Railroad was also thriving from shipments for the Confederate Army. Captain Cullison's fortunes were rising, buoyed by both sides.

The steamboats continue with their routes, although most of them had a least a couple of soldiers on them all the time, as freight and people needed to be taken up and down the bay. The boats continued to stop in Virginia for a while until the Confederacy began to round up crops for their own use and stop letting them be shipped north.

Our buyboat fleet was never busier. When they weren't shooting at each other or running spies across the river, the watermen were out to make a living and continued tonging and soon began dredging. We bought all their catches and took them to market in Washington and Baltimore. We rarely ever went to Norfolk until after the war was over.

***

William continued to excel with his speaking and reading the news. His reading gave more insight as to the effect the war had on the area.

A letter from Leesburg, published in the Richmond Enquirer, says, "at the late battle there, about 30 Confederates were killed, among whom are Clinton Hatcher, of Loudoun County, Donahue, of Loudoun, and a son of Gov. Pettus, of Mississippi. Many are wounded: Lieutenant-Colonel Tebbs of the Eighth Virginia was slightly wounded—grazed on the cheek. Col. Burt of Mississippi was badly wounded in the thigh—not mortally. Dr. Martin of Mississippi was shot through the lungs—supposed to be mortally wounded. Lieut. B. G. Carter, Eighth Virginia, was wounded in the back. Lieut. Fleming had his leg shot off, and Dr. Brock his arm."

Gen. Dix, U. S. A., commanding in Baltimore, has issued a proclamation directing the arrest of all persons in rebellion against the United States, and who may return to the city and appear at the election polls next week, and calling "on all good and loyal citizens to support the judges of election, the United States Marshal and his deputies, and the Provost Marshal of Baltimore, and the police, in their efforts to secure a free and fair expression of the voice of the people of Maryland, and, at the same time, to prevent the ballot boxes from being polluted by treasonable votes."

Of all our old exchange papers from Virginia, we do not now receive a single one.

We do not know, even, if any of our former familiar newspaper acquaintances in the neighboring counties appear "in public" at all—and the other day, when we saw in the Northern papers an extract from the Leesburg Washingtonian, it seemed like hearing of the safety of a friend whom we had supposed list of the dead.

The Northern papers give full accounts of the batteries on the Potomac, extending from Quantico to Aquia Creek. They are represented to be strong in position, with heavy trims, and well manned.

General Scott sent to the President of the United States, on Thursday, a letter announcing his retirement from active service in the Army. He states that the infirmities, some hurts received a few years ago, as a necessity for recruiting his health, compel him to this course. He speaks of pain which he experiences from what he calls "the unnatural and unjust rebellion now raging in the Southern States to our lite prosperous and happy Union;" and he--turns his thanks to the President and Secretary of War, for their uniform kindness to him, and compliments "the patriotism without sectional proclivities or prejudice" of the President.

The letter was read at a Cabinet Meeting, and the request of General Scott complied with. An order was released that the retirement should be made without deduction in Gen. Scott's pay, subsistence, and allowances; and complimenting him in the highest terms.

This order the President and Cabinet carried to the residence of Gen. Scott where it was read to him. He spoke to the President feelingly, reiterating his belief in the patriotism and ability of the administration.

The President made an appropriate reply—and will send Gen. Scott a written letter. The Secretary of War has already addressed him a letter. Gen. Scott will proceed to New York, accompanied by the Secretaries of the Treasury and of War.

He may make a voyage to Europe. Every possible honor has been done him by the Executive.

Gen. McClellan has, in obedience to orders, assumed the command of the Armies of the United States, in place of General Scott, retired, and has issued an address, announcing the acceptance of his new position, and speaking in the most exalted terms of his predecessor. He concludes his proclamation by exhorting the troops "to do nothing hereafter which can cause General Scott to blush for them, but to let their future victories illuminate the close of a life so grand."

Body Found.

—The body of the negro lad Sam, who was drowned in Hunting Creek during the late storm, had been searched for with much care. The exertions for its recovery have been successful, and on yesterday afternoon, the body was found a short distance from the bridge; it showed traces of having laid in the water but was properly cared for and decently interred.

Hunting Creek Bridge.

—This structure which was torn up soon after the U. S. forces occupied this city, but which has lately been reconstructed by Federal workmen, suffered somewhat from the recent flood. A portion of the causeway on each side of the woodwork is washed away, and it will require some filling in to place the bridge in as good condition as it was before the storm. This work will, we presume, be done at once.

The following curious telegraphic dispatch from Alexandria appears in the New York Herald: —"The private correspondence and memoranda of Col. B. Berry, of Virginia, at present an officer of the Confederate army, was discovered and seized at Alexandria on Sunday. Among the articles seized is a full set of regalia of the Order of the Knights of the Golden Circle, of which Berry is said to be a prominent officer.

False Report.

The rumor that on Saturday last, a woman and child were swept from Hunting Creek Bridge and drowned had no foundation.

Foot-Ball.

—This game seems of late to have become

universally popular in this city. On all the streets, in the market, on the wharf— on the commons, everywhere—foot-ball—foot-ball. Men play it, boys play it, and just now, it seems to be "the thing." Pipes and Foot-Balls are having their day. We argue, however, that the game be discarded in all the business streets—so that passersby—especially ladies, be not incommoded by dashing balls and gangs of lads running at full tilt.

The Federal batteries near Budd's Ferry are not far from the water's edge. One has been completed. Sickles' brigade in Maryland has been largely reinforced. Since the storm, we have heard of no military operation on the lower Potomac, either by the land or river forces of the belligerents.

A dispatch dated Savannah, November 12, says there was a fight below that city, originating in consequence of the Federals attempting to burn a vessel aground on Warsaw beach. The attempt failed, and the Federal frigate left.

The Richmond Enquirer announces that it is extremely difficult to obtain a passport to leave the Southern Confederacy or to pass through the lines on any pretense whatever.

The Enquirer has raised the flag of Davis and Stephens, whose re-election it favors.—

The election is set for today.

There is a great scarcity of printing paper at Richmond, and the Enquirer, in consequence, has cut off all subscribers who are in arrears.

The Virginia Fire and Marine Insurance Company have just declared a semi-annual dividend of 10 percent.

The Norfolk Day Book is printed on brown wrapping paper. It is the only paper published in Norfolk and says, as bad as the paper is, it has not enough of it to print more than one-fourth of its edition on.

Over $50,000 worth of clothing has been received at Richmond, voluntarily contributed by citizens of the Confederate States for the benefit of the soldiers.

On Saturday last, there were 1,711 prisoners of war in Richmond. In the last sixteen days, the prisoners there had eaten up $2,000 worth of beef. Since the war commenced, 2,685 prisoners have been brought to Richmond.

The 15th of November has been designated by the Hon. Jeff Davis as a day of fasting, humiliation, and prayer in the Confederate States.

A dispatch from Charleston reports the latest storm as exceedingly violent along the whole Southern coast.

The Louisville Courier of the 29th states that recruiting for the Union cause is an entire failure in portions of Kentucky.

TWELVE - FROZEN RIVERS TO BIG CHANGES

I spent every day but Sundays on the water, as Captain Cullison had adjusted my schedule so that, weather permitting, I could return to Cambridge late on Saturday afternoon.

The bay had frozen over for a few weeks in February of 1863. Just over a year after Molly and I were married, she gave birth to our son. We named our boy after two of his grandfathers—Zachary Aaron Douglas.

My grandfather was still getting along all right, and my brother William had seen much of the bloodletting of war while the *Savannah* ferried troops injured in the Battle of Manassas down the Potomac, from Washington to the Hammond Hospital at Point Lookout. He soon lost the lust to join the Rebs in Virginia. Instead, he began to do double duty in relieving Willy at the helm and learning from my grandfather how to navigate the bay and all the rivers. John was catching on to the "family business" of being a newsreader. My mother let him stay on year-round with Grandpa because the war had forced the school in Leesburg to close.

William, assisted by John, continued to establish the position of a newsreader as one of great importance, which was being copied on other steamships. The service was popular with the travelers, and it provided the *Savannah* with a competitive advantage.

John had been working as William's understudy. In addition to being able to recite Shakespeare and read the newspapers, he played the banjo, which was quite popular among the passengers. Even with the musical addition, John kept the hard news flowing to the passengers with this update:

***

In the afternoon, the Cameron Light Guard

paraded and were reviewed by a committee from the city of Philadelphia who had come to Washington to present a word to Gen. McClellan. Col. Lewis T. Wigfall, lately Senator from Texas, has been promoted to the rank of Brigadier-General of the Confederate Army.

Extracts from Richmond papers to the 29th Oct. are given in the Northern papers. They do not contain much news. Accounts are given of the battle of Edward's Ferry and of the arrival at Richmond of numerous prisoners taken in that battle. The names of twenty-two commissioned officers are given, among which are those of Colonels Lee and Cogswell and the two Reveres.

Two letters from Dumfries, on the Lower Potomac, are given, from which it would appear that active operations have been going on in that quarter and that the batteries below Aquia Creek are defended by a strong supporting force. Contributions to the fund for furnishing supplies to the Maryland Regiment appear to have been made to a liberal extent.

The New Orleans Crescent says, "There have been large remittances from Tennessee in treasury notes within the past few days to be invested in sugar and molasses. The demand for sugar and molasses for Alabama and Tennessee is extending, and heavy transactions are expected the present month."

Gen. A. S. Johnston has been placed in command of all the Confederate forces in Missouri and has issued a proclamation forbidding any property leaving the State.

The special Washington correspondent of the New York Tribune, under date of Friday, telegraphs as follows. "It is understood that the naval expedition is not directed at cities on or near the Southern coast. The troops will land at thinly settled locations, with spacious harbors, and will open cotton ports and establish a basis of operation for additional forces now training" Beaufort, N. C, Fernandina, and other places are named in other papers, as places for debarkation.

At Edwards' and Conrad's Ferries on Sunday, all remained quiet. A day or two ago, a large encampment of Confederates was encamped near the villa of Hon. Thos. Swann, formerly Mayor of Baltimore, but on the following morning, it had disappeared. Mr. Swann's residence is near Leesburg and in full view of Edward's Ferry, and from its tower can be observed every strategic point for many miles. It is not unlikely that it has long been used by the Confederates as an observation post.

The New York Herald of yesterday says- "We learn from St. Louis, on the authority of a loyal citizen just returned from the camp of General Price, at Neosho, Newtown County, that the latter general and Ben McCulloch had united their forces- 30,000 strong—at that place. Large quantities of clothes, medicine, and other supplies had reached, and he expected a number of rifled cannon to arrive, in charge of Gen. George B Clark. It was said that Price intended to give Fremont battle at Neosho, where he hoped to defeat him, and then march on St. Louis and make his winter quarters in Central Missouri."

A distinguished physician, who died some years since in Paris, declared: "I believe that during the twenty-six years I have practiced my profession in this city, 20 000 children have been carried to the cemeteries a sacrifice to the absurd custom of exposing their arms and necks."

Report From The Naval Expedition.

When the steamer Georgiana left Old Point on Saturday evening, it was reported that one of the government steamers, having on board upwards of eight hundred soldiers, had been wrecked some thirty miles south of Cape Hatteras and that only one hundred and fifty men were saved.

Another vessel, loaded with cattle, had been blown onshore, and the few cattle that were not drowned escaped into the interior. The Government steamer George Peabody, which had made harbor in Hampton Roads, dragged her anchors during the gale and was onshore at Hampton Bar. Several steamers were engaged during Saturday, endeavoring to get her off, but without success. The weather in the lower part of the bay and on the coast is reported to have been equally as severe as any experienced for a number of years. A steamer with a flag of truce, which left Old Point for Norfolk on Friday, was compelled to make a harbor at Sewall's Point and had not returned up to Saturday night. We shall doubtless be shortly compelled to record much loss and suffering from vessels on the coast.

The Wharf after the Flood

—The Potomac subsided considerably on Sunday, but on Monday sunk to within a short distance of its ordinary high water level. The strand along the river, however, exhibited as many evidences of the passing of the waters as the land of Egypt after the Nile's embrace. The embankment of the Alexandria, Loudoun, and Hampshire Railroad, crossing the low grounds, was somewhat washed by the influx of waters but may easily be repaired. Fishtown, as usual, has been partly floated away—piles of timber, grass, and detritus mark the path of the waters. The bed of the Orange Railroad, from Queen to Prince Street, has been damaged and will, at Borne points, soon require to be relayed. At the foot of all the streets, there is a deposit of rich mud, varying from five inches to half an inch in thickness. Some of the lower store floors are located in a like manner. Some of the timbers of the Long Wharf have been torn away, and Hunter's Wharf, near the lower plaster mill, is almost bare of planking. The other wharves have suffered but slightly. To this morning, however, the traces of the flood were in most places nearly obliterated.

Wood—We call the attention of our readers to

the advertisement of Mr. B. T. Plummer, which appears in another column of today's News. Those who want of an excellent article of wood could do no better thing than to leave their orders with him at once.

Small vessels occasionally continue to come up the river, either by hugging the Maryland shore, passing the batteries in the night, or being allowed to sail by unmolested.

It is impossible for us, in our limited space, and with this small sheet, to publish long articles; and, besides, in these times, if they could be printed, they would not be read.—

We have to condense, in the shortest possible space, the current news, of which we must keep a daily record, and the local items—often compressing the whole columns of words of the large newspapers into real substance contained in what the printers call a stick full, and laboring to present the "age and body of the times, their form and pressure," within the limits to which we are now curtailed, and we hope all our citizens every Alexandrian, will generously aid us in our efforts to present them daily this little home paper, until the opening of the mails, to the southern counties, the revival of business, and the condition of public affairs will allow us to recommence again the publication of the old Alexandria Gazette in its former proportions.

From the official report of the proceedings which occurred between General Stone and General McClellan preceding the battle at Ball's Bluff, it would appear that there was some misapprehension on the part of General Stone as to the precise meaning of the order sent to him by General McClellan. It is evident that the latter officer had no intention to order General Stone to cross the Potomac, but it seems that the instructions to keep a lookout on Leesburg, and to make a demonstration, so as to distract the Confederates, while General McCall was advancing from Drainsville, was construed into an order to throw his troops across into Virginia.

***

We had a hard freeze, and instead of the ice cracking up and letting things move around a bit, everyone was stuck at the dock. The Navy had a couple of ironclad ships, and some oyster sloops had copper wrapping on their hulls, mainly to cover seams to make them hold up until their next hauling. Few boats went anywhere for six weeks until the early March thaw began to free up the boats. But while they were locked solid, the Yankees had a hard time keeping up with Confederate supply lines moving back and forth across the Potomac. Men were moving at night and crossing the river in as little as an hour in some cases. Wary of thin ice, the rebels had devised ingenious ways to skim over the ice with sails. If they hit patches of water, they simply floated until the next solid ice, when their "iceboat" would fly with the wind to the other shore. Of course, those who simply tried to walk or even ride a horse across sometimes vanished, never to be heard from again.

A Yankee patrol decided one day to try to catch an ice skimmer, and they took off on their mounts, ripping along at full gallop until the ice gave way under them, and they all sank quickly. The horses tried desperately to make it to shore, but they couldn't get back up and soon ran out of energy. It was an awful waste of good horses. The news article in which I read about that incident made no mention of the loss of the Yankee soldiers. Worse yet, the Union Army had seized the horses from farmers near Leonardtown. They had a detachment of soldiers assigned permanently to the area after Congressman Benjamin Harris, a resident of the town, had been arrested for giving aid and comfort to the enemy. That detachment was now lacking six soldiers, and the owners of the horses would never be paid.

Southern Maryland was firmly part of the South, and its proximity to Washington always worried those at the headquarters of the Army in Washington. The headquarters had stationed over thirty thousand troops in St. Mary's, and Charles counties as worries about Confederate invasions continued. The arrest of the popular Congressman only made matters worse. John made a lot of passengers nervous when he informed them that one of their neighbors' entire family had been arrested for lying to federal troops trying to track down

Confederates.

***

This report appeared in a newspaper:

By order of Brigadier General Sickles, a family consisting of husband, wife, and daughters were arrested near Port Tobacco and brought to Washington. They are confined in the jail at Seventeenth Street, charged with harboring Confederates and giving information detrimental to the interests of the Federal army.

***

The war wasn't going well for the North, which had experienced a string of defeats, and Lincoln continued to change commanders. Summer came and with it a major invasion of the north by General Robert E. Lee. The newspapers began to scream about Lincoln's ineptness in conducting the war. The bloody days at Gettysburg sent the Confederates reeling back to Virginia, but the battle was no real picnic for the North either. It was, in fact, a costly victory. For those of us on the Bay, it meant that, while still technically part of the North, we were viewed with a great deal of suspicion. Many Union troops and naval commanders were decent and honorable, but of course, there were legions of those who weren't.

The war wore on into early 1865. It finally ended with General Lee's surrender to General Grant. We were soon overrun with carpetbaggers, who were all friends of the politicians in Washington. But life was much worse in Virginia and the rest of the South.

The *Maryland Lady* continued to move great quantities of fish, crabs, and oysters to market. All six of Captain Cullison's buyboats survived the war, with mine the most profitable. By the end of the war, I was twenty-five, and Molly had given us another child. When I went to Captain Cullison's office at Cobb Island the week after Yankee troops had swarmed over the area looking for the assassins of President Lincoln, he had a surprise for me.

"Lad, I am going to sell you the buyboats. All six of them," he said. "I have no need of them. My stocks in the railroads have all done well, as have yours. I am going to relax a little bit, and since I have no sons that I can turn over my business to, I am going to sell it to you at a fair price and at which you can make a handsome profit. You are the best captain I have had in forty years. I am going to La Plata today to see Mr. Mudd, my attorney, and he will draw up the papers for us. Be here next Monday, and we will sign it over to you."

"Captain, I don't know how I can come up with the money to pay you on such short notice," I said.

"Don't worry, lad. You need nothing to pay down, and I will finance the entire cost. You have earned this consideration."

Captain Cullison was true to his word, and within two years, I had paid him off fully and owned a fleet of buyboats at the age of twenty-seven. Molly and I also had a third son. William was itching to take over as captain of the *Savan-*

nah, but Grandpa said that at twenty-two, he was too young for such a major responsibility. Therefore, Grandpa gave him the title of First Officer, a position that the steamboat never had before, and it seemed to satisfy William. John was turning out to be quite a ham and was gaining a bit of a following for his dramatic enactments of the news in the grand salon of the *Savannah*. I had my eye on my brothers and knew that they would be safe with Grandpa carefully watching them, but he was about the oldest captain on the bay. I planned to make my move and bring my brothers to work with me when Grandpa decided to step aside. My mother and my three youngest siblings, sisters Evelyn and Betty and brother Allen, had moved to Cambridge to be near Molly and our children.

William rarely had time to fill in as the newsreader due to his new position on the ship. John continued to establish the position of a newsreader as one of great importance and which was being copied on other steamships. The service was popular with the travelers and provided the *Savannah* with a competitive advantage since it was the first and thus the most fabled.

Guns protected the City of Washington at Hunting Creek.

USS Polaris at the Washington Navy Yard

THE ASSASSINATION OF PRESIDENT LINCOLN.

THIRTEEN – DEATH OF A PRESIDENT

The uproar over the murder of President Lincoln had brought new terror to the Potomac region, southern Maryland, and Virginia. 'The boot of the despot's heel,' which had been ground into the State of Maryland, resonated in song as the lyrics of "Maryland, My Maryland."

Maryland had not been a part of the Union any more than the Confederate states, even though it had not seceded, but it was territory held by Union troops. There were over thirty thousand troops alone in southern Maryland, which was the path of escape for the murderer of the president.

For many in the Old Line State, the presence of a military government began to transition back to a civilian government in the months following the end of the war. We began to see fewer Naval vessels stopping and searching our buyboats or harassing the steamboats. They were no longer looking for Confederate spies. With the war over, the chief danger on the bay and the Potomac returned to piracy and oyster wars.

The role of a buyboat, as was my business, was to simply provide an easy and accessible market for the watermen so they could stay over top of the oyster bars and continue to pull up oysters off the bottom.

The steamboat business was flourishing. Now that the war had been over for several years, new ships were under construction. The *Savannah* was nearing the end of her life, as was Grandpa. He still worked, but in the role of Fleet Admiral, as the Norfolk and Baltimore line wouldn't let him completely retire.

William was more than able to take over as captain, but Grandpa had lived the last thirty-five years on the *Savannah* and didn't want to waste away the rest of his time on earth sitting on a rocking chair on dry land. Thus, William became Captain Douglas. Grandpa traveled along too but spent more time in the grand saloon socializing with the passengers. He found he liked the very different role and was able to greet people he had known over the years. He also got a kick out of listening to John as the current newsreader. John was the biggest ham in the family and loved the job. We all knew he was destined to be an actor. John had different ideas, which was why he was training Allen to be the newsreader on the *Savannah*. He told me one day that he wanted to open a newspaper in Washington. He asked me to help him find the money to do it.

"John, what in the world qualifies you to run a newspaper?" I asked him.

"I have been reading the newspapers for more than eight years. I have spotted all their mistakes and figured out how they were either incomplete or simply incompetent. I can't do any worse than the ones already in business. I just might do a lot better."

I talked to Captain Cullison and Grandpa, and they both had the same answer. There was no way on God's green earth that I could talk John out of following his passion. He had demonstrated a keen knowledge of the news business, so we all ought to get behind him with the money he needed to open his own newspaper. So we did.

Captain Cullison had a friend who owned a fine three-story building around the corner from

Mrs. Surratt's boarding house in Washington. The neighborhood had become famous following the assassination of President Lincoln. Mrs. Surratt had been hung along with the men involved, the execution taking place but a block from the U. S. Capitol. When I saw the picture in the newspaper of Mrs. Surratt being hung, I was reminded of the day I had seen the slaves auctioned off not far from the Capitol building.

To me, it looked like I had little chance of bringing William to work in my seafood business, as he was well-liked by the steamboat company. William was making good money, and he was sweet on Molly's cousin. I could sense a wedding in the offing. John had decided on a different path from William and me. Since both were industrious, I knew they would do well. I still had my sisters Evelyn and Betty and my youngest brother, Allen, to bring along. My mother, with all of her children grown, was spending so much time helping Molly with our children that we fixed up more space for her to live with us. Our large home on the Choptank River had many rooms, which we were doing our best to fill with babies. We were soon to have Grandpa with us for a while.

CHESAPEAKE 1850

The boarding house of Mary Surratt in Washington, D.C.

FOURTEEN - GOOD FORTUNES

"Well, my dear brother, what will be the headline today?" John looked up from papers he was reading on his desk as I strolled into the office unannounced. *The Washington Herald* was in full bloom, with newspapers being hawked by boys in several locations on street corners as I walked over to John's office from the wharves. My visit was unannounced because his receptionist, my sister Betty, had been sent on an errand to listen to a congressional hearing on the administration of federal territories and the latest Indian wars.

"Where is everyone?" I asked.

"Well, other than Betty on Capitol Hill, I have a reporter who followed fire wagons up Georgia Avenue, one who took the train to Rockville for a murder trial, and another who is in line at the White House to try to talk to President Grant about a scandal in his administration."

"Well, John, it looks like you won't run out of news, but who is out around the city selling advertising?"

"Aunt Cecile has proven to be a formidable businesswoman, and she has hired a staff of six ad salesmen who are doing so well; we are now printing three editions every day."

"Are you making money?"

"Evelyn is my bookkeeper, and she reports that by the end of this year, we will begin paying dividends to you and our other investors. So, yes, dear brother, you and I, Grandpa, and Captain Cullison are all making money."

Washington had changed considerably since I first visited with Grandpa on the *Savannah*. Twenty years had seen the Washington Monument finally completed, many new buildings built along the city's grand avenues, and a streetcar line branching out in every direction. The crooks were taking advantage of the naivety of President Grant, who, while he could win a war, wasn't able to show many victories in peace. But the newspapers all said he was so popular that he would surely win another term. His pals were likely to have stolen the last public dollar, but the voters didn't seem either to care or to expect any different.

Molly's father was still serving in Congress and, in fact, had decided to run for governor. As my seafood business had expanded to running a wholesale market in Baltimore and one in Washington, I had my hands full. I really wished I had some of my family working with me, but except for William and Allen, they were working for John. While my captains and crews were all good people, I still envied my younger brother, who was able to keep his family close to him at work.

I began taking off each weekend as our children grew older, and I only took the helm of a buy-boat to relieve a captain.

The Norfolk railroad was back in full operation, and my stock was making as much money for me as the Pennsylvania and the B&O.

Captain Cullison had talked me into investing in the C&O. My wealth soared, and my seafood was delivered in fresh ice to all of the major railroads and shipped up and down the East Coast and as far west as Chicago. I had sent a young fellow to major hotels in each city to engage them for our oyster packing house, and we became the largest oyster seller east of the Mississippi. It had been a long time since I'd gone to work for Captain Cullison. I treasured his guidance as much as that of Grandpa.

FIFTEEN –THE FOURTH AND FAMILY AFFAIRS

John marked his first anniversary in business with a large party for the Fourth of July at his new home on the bluff overlooking the Potomac River at Georgetown. It had been a long trip for all of us to travel by steamboat to Washington, but for Grandpa, it had been a long time coming. He had retired three years earlier, and his delicate health had kept him from any trips on the Savannah for the past year. William was able to arrange for a substitute captain and all of our family, including William's new bride, attended John's celebration.

Even Molly's father, the new Governor of Maryland, attended, as did many congressmen and senators. John's newspaper had gained mightily in popularity and rivaled the six other newspapers in the nation's capital. John didn't forget his roots, and he sent bundles of newspapers to all the trains heading out of town three times daily.

He had agents line up newsstand dealers in other cities, and soon the *Washington Herald* became a newspaper that readers turned to when they wanted to know what was being done and debated in Washington. John also had several newspapers delivered to each of the steamboats that came to the wharves in Washington and Alexandria. His sales manager made it a point to visit each ship upon docking and give the newsreader a tip for giving favorable play to the *Washington Herald*.

Each of the steamship lines had copied the *Savannah*'s newsreader position. Some of the most prominent of the newsreaders gained a following, and they were able to make the steamboat companies bid for their services.

I had sent twenty bushels of blue crabs to John's house for his cooks to steam for the party. His cooks had been frying chicken since early in the morning. With large bowls of fresh potato salad, iced tea, lemonade, fresh corn on the cob, and platters of fresh-sliced tomatoes, the spread was great Chesapeake Bay fare. John even had a champion oyster shucker providing fresh oysters to those who wanted to partake.

John invited Governor Taylor to speak, and, in view of the warming sun, he was mercifully short. Fourth of July parties were always a mixed barrel of emotions for Molly, who could never forget that her grandfather had taken ill and died after a similar event twenty years earlier.

John's house was large enough for all of the family to stay for the weekend. With Aunt Cecile running his business office, our sister Evelyn as his bookkeeper, and our other sister as his secretary and receptionist, the newspaper had taken off like a rocket. John was able to purchase his fine new home at a great price when it had come on the market after an elderly former senator from Tennessee died.

The senator's family had moved back to their home state and had no use for the house in Washington, which they viewed as a nuisance. John provided for his sisters as well, finding a nice home for them on Wisconsin Avenue, where they lived with our aunt. She acted as a house mother for them, as both were pretty and were being courted by various suitors.

At about midnight, Grandpa hollered, and a loud thud emanated from the room where he had been sleeping.

When I got to his room, he was gone. He must have had a heart attack because he was quiet and still on the floor without any sign of life. Our moment of celebration for John's newspaper and the nation's birthday had taken a new turn, and I wondered if I would ever again be able to talk Molly into going to another Fourth of July party. I made it clear to everyone the next morning that we had nothing to grieve about because Grandpa had made it to eighty-four years of age, and each day had been happy and healthy.

We buried Grandpa on a hill overlooking the steamboat landing in Cambridge, a place where he said he wanted to be. I owned the farm and the land where he was buried, and we decided to allocate the site as a family graveyard. Grandpa was at peace, and the sounds of the steamboat whistles signaling when they left the dock were all the music that he needed to hear. We had all traveled to Cambridge the day after he died to bury him. Molly hosted everyone at our house for a few days, and we continued the party where we had left off.

Now that Molly's father and mother were living in the Governor's Mansion in Annapolis, she and the children, which had grown in number to four, would take the steamboat from Cambridge to visit. They would take along my mother as well, and all of the womenfolk got along famously. Their trips were as much an adventure as ever. They would stay in Annapolis for a week or so in the summer when the children were out of school or on breaks.

SIXTEEN - RENEWED OYSTER WAR ON THE BAY

The next winter found my business on the Chesapeake prosperous but in peril. The watermen continued to fight and kill one another, and the newspapers were making a big ruckus out of it because they hadn't anything better to do. Soon the legislators were demanding that Governor Taylor take action, and thus the Maryland Oyster Navy was born.

It was important that my buyboat captains follow two important rules. The first was not to take sides between the watermen. Our business was to buy the catch of any waterman, regardless of their family, their port, or their state, or even to question the legality of the way or the location of where the oysters were harvested. The second rule was that when the shooting started, our boats were under orders to run as fast and as far from the bloodshed as possible and never to fire unless fired upon.

The watermen, better to call many of them pirates—they even preferred that term—were fortifying themselves with larger ordnance than in prior years. That year there were reports of cannon being mounted on skipjacks, and recently one of them had fired on a new Oyster Navy boat. The Oyster Navy boat fired back, and one policeman and two pirates had been killed.

All of the newspapers in Baltimore and Annapolis, as well as the cities up and down the East Coast, began telling the story of the lawlessness on the Chesapeake. My brother John's newspaper had some of the more vivid coverage, with embellishments that carried the story a little too far. I pointed out that while three dead was tragic, his newspaper had suggested that there might have been more men killed who fell into the bay, and if the crabs ate their dead bodies, we might never know the true body count. The truth of the matter was that had any others been killed and gone overboard, their bodies would float up in a few weeks and only be nibbled on; most of the crabs dug down in the mud in the winter and weren't feeding.

"Thank you, big brother. I will be glad to advise the reporter to nose around down in Crisfield and see if he can't find someone to watch for floating bodies," John said.

"I want to see this newspaper excel, John. You have been mightily successful, and the way to continue to do so is to keep the trust of your readers."

"Okay, Ethan. I'm listening, big brother. Evelyn gave me the same talk this morning. Until we dig up some more information on the Oyster Wars, I think we can tone it down a bit."

"John, I'm fearful that things are going to get a lot worse out on the open waters as these characters fight over the oysters. It's big money these days, and there is a mindset among them that they don't mind spilling blood."

All through the winter, battles raged on the waters of the Potomac and the Chesapeake. By spring, there were at least two dozen killed in the war for the "white gold." Come spring, there would be a relative calm, as the fighting over crabs and fish was nothing to write home about. The competition over them was nothing at all like the Oyster Wars.

Maryland had outlawed dredging due to the process allowing oystermen to simply harvest every oyster in existence. Only tonging was allowed in Maryland, but Virginia still allowed dredging until 1879. Virginia, strapped for cash, sold its three-boat maritime police fleet and was unable to enforce its rules and laws.

Thus, Maryland oyster pirates were slipping into Virginia waters during the night to dredge. The situation prompted the Governor of Virginia to order his state militia onto a fleet of boats to raid the pirates as they worked.

The first such raid ordered by Governor William Cameron in 1882 found forty-six oyster pirates. They were convicted on charges of violating Virginia's oystering laws.

The governor's fleet included a tug and a freighter, and he engaged the pirates at the mouth of the Rappahannock River. Seven boats were seized, and many of the pirates were from Maryland. A year later, when the governor's popularity began to sink, he organized another expedition to hunt down the oyster pirates, and this time he brought along the press.

As someone who got his start by reading newspapers, I was heartened to read the account in the *Norfolk Virginian*. The paper reported that one of the governor's ships had no ballast, and when it ran into heavy seas, began pitching and tossing so violently that the assembled military officers were tossed back and forth along with the ship's coal stove, which badly burned several of the men. Many became seasick. The goal of the expedition was to seize the crowd of pirates near Smith Point, some of whom the governor had pardoned after the raid the year before.

Instead of nabbing the rumored fifty or sixty such pirate ships dredging oysters, there were but eight. Governor Cameron's fleet opened fire with twenty-four cannons and hundreds of muskets, but none hit anything. Only one pirate boat was captured, the *Palo Alto* of Crisfield, Maryland. She was unable to outrun the Virginia posse, but the *Palo Alto's* captain and mate were able to escape in a rowboat. Not only were the Maryland pirates laughing at the governor, so were all the newspapers that he didn't take with him on the raid. Even the ungrateful reporters who he did ask to accompany him on the raid poked fun at his efforts. The Norfolk Academy of Music put on a comic opera that lampooned the governor's raid. Oysters from the Chesapeake were supplying half the world's demand, and my seafood distribution company was dominating the business.

John did what he said he would and sent a reporter over to Crisfield on Maryland's Eastern Shore to hire on as a hand on an oyster boat. His man was one of those who were illegally dredging oysters when Governor Cameron's fleet raided them at Smith Point. John's newspaper account several days later was one of the more hilarious reports, noting that the fleeing Maryland boats were more than a half-mile away when the Virginia fleet opened fire. The entire barrage of cannonballs and bullets fell far short of their boats.

John was learning the newspaper business and doing a good job, and I decided to stop giving him advice.

Oyster Police overtaking oyster pirates on the Chesapeake Bay. Frank Leslie Illustrated News

SEVENTEEN - A SUNDAY PICNIC

The First Baptist Church of Roland Park organized a large excursion from Baltimore City to Sandy Point beach for the second Sunday of June. The members of the church, their families, and many friends all arrived at the inner harbor and boarded the steamboat *Crisfield*. The trip was to take about an hour and a half, and the group would land at the beach for a day of picnicking, praying, and swimming. Before the day was over, a lot of the last two would take place.

By nine o'clock that morning, the group had left Pier Seven and was headed south. A sudden explosion took place in a steam boiler, and it shook the *Crisfield* to her rafters. A fire quickly ensued, which was far beyond the capability of anyone to extinguish. Life jackets were quickly passed around to passengers, while the flames and smoke quickly caught the attention of other ships. The steamboat *Northland* began to make way from her position about two miles to the south of the *Crisfield*.

The fire grew quickly, and passengers were donning the life vests and jumping into the bay. The waters were warm, and the ship was about a half-mile from shore. The bay was fairly shallow in that area. The passengers began their frantic swim toward the shoreline and found about halfway to the shore that they could actually walk on the bottom.

Many could not swim and were scared of the water. They were unable to jump into the bay waters, which had already become warm from the late spring sun. Panic enveloped those left on the ship as the water was dotted with people crying for help and swimming. The only two lifeboats on the ship were on the roof of the vessel and couldn't be reached.

The normal capacity of the *Crisfield* was two hundred and fifty, but for a day excursion, the ship was carrying twice that number. There were enough life vests, but many of them were old and rotted, while others could not be reached because they had already been consumed by fire. The fire continued to spread.

The *Northland* arrived while the *Crisfield* was fully involved, and the last passengers and crew were jumping to keep from being burned to death. Every manner of an object was being used by the passengers and crew of the *Northland* to fish people out of the bay. Dozens were walking in the chest-deep water, heading for shore. Many bodies of those without life vests were floating, and the *Crisfield* continued to burn. Small pleasure boats and fishing boats that had been working on a Sunday morning also arrived to pluck survivors out of the bay.

***

I read the account in John's newspaper as I sat down for breakfast at my office in Baltimore. There had been 510 people on board, including the crew. Of that number, there were now 329 confirmed dead. Most of the survivors were uninjured, but a few had suffered burns. It had taken several days to accumulate and account for the survivors because they had been taken to different locations by the various boats that had come to their aid.

The Maryland Oyster Navy had also spent several days picking up bodies from the water. Fishermen and crabbers helped in the effort.

The following Sunday, a church service was held. Friends and families of those who were on board gathered at the church in Baltimore to give thanks for those who survived and ask for deliverance into Heaven for those who did not.

An editorial in John's newspaper asked the question about fire safety on steamboats and why so many people were allowed to crowd onto the ships for Sunday excursions. What lessons would be learned about making the ships less likely to burn so fast?

The newspaper cited the old and rotted life jackets on the *Crisfield* as the chief cause of so many drownings and which failed to support those who were able to get them on. The loss of life was the largest in Baltimore since the War Between the States had ended.

With passengers inspecting the life vests themselves on other steamboats, orders for replacements numbering in the thousands poured into several small factories in Baltimore and Washington, which sewed and manufactured the vests.

One such factory belonged to my Aunt Cecile. She and her sister Gussie, both sisters of my late father, had moved to Washington from Georgia a few years earlier, and Cecile had been working with John.

After assisting John with the newspaper, she had used her savings to buy a small sewing and tailoring business. Her ability to attract customers and manage her help had led to great growth, and she began producing life vests for all of the steamboat companies anxious to replace their old vests. She soon was custom-making draperies for the fine homes and embassies of Washington.

A sideline was custom ladies' undergarments. As girdles were popular for ladies of girth, she began to manufacture clothing that was sold in the finest ladies' shops and department stores in Washington.

EIGHTEEN – A NEW LINE

William had been successful, too, and over the years had attained a record of fidelity and demonstrated ability for the Norfolk and Baltimore line. Captain Cullison wrote me a letter about a month after the *Crisfield* disaster and asked me to meet with him at Cobb Island.

"Why don't you buy the Norfolk and Baltimore

line, Ethan? It's a good company and well-run, but stocks are down for steamship companies right now, and you can buy a controlling interest in it for a bargain. If you buy it, I will join you in the investment. My guess is that if we both put up two million dollars each, we can end up with at least fifty-five percent of the stock."

"I don't have time to run the company, Captain. Do you have someone in mind?"

"I sure do. Your brother William is as solid a man as any."

"I admit he is a good fellow with a sharp mind, but running a steamship and running a fleet are two different things."

"Aha, my lad, you did just fine taking over my fleet at a young age, and William is quite a bit older than you were when you became proprietor of Cullison Seafood. Look what you have done with it over the years. You have done things I had never thought to do, and now the company is the top wholesaler in the east."

"Imagine what Grandpa would say, from cabin boy and newsreader to owning the steamship company," I replied. "I know you are right. William is capable, and I always wanted him to work with me. He always wanted to stay with the steamship line. I shall join with you, Captain Cullison, and we shall name William as president of the line. I expect we will have a hard time getting him into the main office, though. He loves being on the water."

"Ethan, that's an advantage to have the person in charge that knows every detail of the operations. He will do fine."

The next day, Captain Cullison and I traveled to Norfolk and bought the Norfolk and Baltimore line. In fact, we bought all the stock because of the lack of interest following the *Crisfield* fire. The first item of business was to place orders for lifeboats and new life vests, and of course, the vests were ordered from Aunt Cecile. The second decision was to replace the aging *Savannah* with a new ship. The plans were drawn up by William, and after a few discussions with Captain Cullison, the order for the replacement of the *Savannah* was given to a Baltimore shipyard. It would be ready in ten months and would be named the *Captain Douglas*.

Grandpa would have laughed about having a ship named after him. But his photo would be the centerpiece of the ship's grand saloon.

Even though he had passed, he would continue to live on as the Admiral of the Chesapeake Bay.

The End

CHESAPEAKE 1850

Steamboat arrives at Mount Vernon,
home of President George Washington.
Library of Congress.

Interior of steamboat passenger cabin on a Norfolk and Washington line steamer.

Headquarters of Capt. A. G. Lee in Alexandria, Va.

Excavating for track connection at Devereaux Station for the Orange and Alexandria railroad.

Lincoln's inauguration in 1865. Harpers Weekly

The entrance of Fort Washington guards the approach to the capital along the Potomac River.

Cannon along the walls of Fort Washington on the Potomac River.

CHESAPEAKE 1850

Mary Surratts Boarding House used by conspirators to plan for murder of Lincoln. The building now houses a Chinese Restaurant in China Town.

New railroad bridge being constructed over the Potomac River for the Washington, Alexandria, and Fredericksburg Railroad.

Men are working on scraping the river bottom for oysters with the long-handled tongs, right, and culling the oysters to retain the mature ones and send small ones back to the river.

Oyster pirates dredging at night on the Chesapeake Bay.

Harpers Weekly

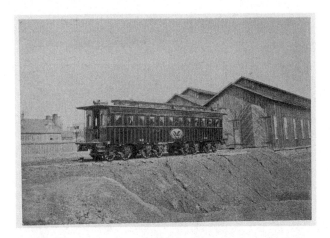

President Abraham Lincoln's personal railroad car was stored at Alexandria, Virginia, railroad yard. The car was later used to carry his coffin back to Illinois following his murder.

Union Navy prepares for expeditions against Confederacy along Atlantic coast.

CHESAPEAKE 1850

Officers and men on the Union Monitor, warship

Freight ready to load on steamboats.

Hooray for Abe and the Union! F.C. Yohn.

ENTER TODAY with your EMAIL address for a chance to win a FREE PAPERWHITE KINDLE or Fire Tablet

Visit ThePrivateerClause.com and submit your name and email address and win a free Kindle book along with a chance to win a great new Paperwhite

MORE BOOKS BY KEN ROSSIGNOL

Available In Kindle, Paperback, Hardcover, And Audible At Amazon And Retailers Worldwide

Additional books by Ken Rossignol

Chesapeake 1850
Chesapeake 1880
Chesapeake 1910

Twentieth Century History

SPANISH INFLUENZA - The Story of the Epidemic That Swept America From the Newspaper Reports of 1918

Panama 1914 The Early Years of the Big Dig

Titanic 1912 The original news reporting of the sinking of the Titanic

Titanic & Lusitania- Survivor Stories (with Bruce M.Caplan)

Titanic Poetry, Music & Stories

KLAN: Killing America

Leopold & Loeb Killed Bobby Franks (with Bruce M. Caplan)

SINS OF HER FATHER: Pelosi's Pop Liked Racists and Had High Praise for Fascist Mussolini

Battle of Solomon's Island

The Story of The Rag

Cheap Shots: THE EDITORIAL CARTOONS OF ST. MARY'S TODAY: The Story of The Rag

True Crime

MURDER USA: True Crime, Real Killers

MURDER CHESAPEAKE: True Crime, Real Killers

CHESAPEAKE TRUE CRIME - Top Stories from The Chesapeake Today

The Chesapeake Short Stories Collection

The Chesapeake: Tales & Scales (with Larry Jarboe)

The Chesapeake: Legends, Yarns & Barnacles (with Larry Jarboe)

[The Chesapeake: Oyster Buyboats, Ships & Steamed Crabs](#)
[THE CHESAPEAKE: A Man Born to Hang, Can Never Drown](#)
[THE CHESAPEAKE: Country Cornpone Cornucopia](#)
[THE CHESAPEAKE: Tidewater Sagas](#)

Cruising the Waterfront Restaurants of the Potomac
Coke Air: Chesapeake Crime Confidential

Piracy

Pirate Trials: Dastardly Deeds & Last Words
Pirate Trials: Hung by the Neck Until Dead
Pirate Trials: Famous Murderous Pirates Book Series: THE LIVES AND ADVENTURES of FAMOUS and SUNDRY PIRATES
PIRATE TRIALS: The Three Pirates - Famous Murderous Pirate Books Series: The Islet of the Virgin

The Traveling Cheapskate Series:

The Ninety-Nine Cent Tour of Bar Harbor Maine

Boating Chesapeake Bay

CRUISE FACTS - TRUTH & TIPS ABOUT CRUISE

TRAVEL (Traveling Cheapskate Series Book 2)

ABOUT THE AUTHOR

Ken Rossignol

As a maritime history speaker, Rossignol enjoys meeting audiences around the world and discussing the original news stories of the sinking of the RMS Titanic and other maritime history topics.
Traveling the high seas around the world is the way that the author keeps in touch with the adventures of the Sea Empress and keeps the voyages interesting and the stories coming.
In recent years Rossignol has appeared on dozens of ships in the Pacific, Atlantic, Mediterranean, and the Caribbean discussing the stories of the

history of the Panama Canal, the heroes of the Titanic, the explorations of the new world voyagers, the Bermuda Triangle and the history of piracy, among other maritime history topics.

Rossignol appears at the Titanic Museum Attractions in Pigeon Forge, Tennessee and Branson, Missouri for book signings and to talk with visitors about the RMS Titanic.

With a recent visit to the International Book Fair 2016 in Panama as one of the United States Delegation authors and entertainers Rossignol enjoyed telling the stories of the History of the Panama Canal, Piracy and of the heroes of the Titanic.

He has appeared on Good Morning America, ABC 20/20; ABC World News Tonight and in a 2012 production of Discovery Channel Investigation Motives & Murders Series, A Body in the Bay.

Rossignol's landmark First Amendment case, represented by Levine Sullivan Koch & Schulz re: United States Fourth Circuit Court of Appeals Rossignol v Voorhaar, 2003, spelled out that public officials cannot retaliate against a publisher for criticism of their official acts.

BOOKS BY THIS AUTHOR

Chesapeake 1880: Steamboats & Oyster Wars - The Newsreader (Book Two)

Life in the Chesapeake region for the family of Ethan Aaron Douglas, from steamboats to newspapers, struggles of immigrants and the changes brought by the industrial revolution. The simple life of watermen and challenges of weather, fire and disaster in the era of 1880 to 1910 brought to life for the reader from a life-long resident of the Tidewater region. Catch up on the latest events from around the Chesapeake as told by the NEWS READERS on the steamboats of the Old Bay Line to the passengers.

Chesapeake 1910: News Readers On Bay Steamers, The Great War And Prohibition (Steamboats & Oyster Wars: The News Reader Book 3)

THE THIRD BOOK IN THE CHESAPEAKE SERIES

- Roaring into the Twentieth Century, the Ethan Douglas family faces new challenges with furious weather on the Chesapeake Bay, oyster wars, Titanic and Lusitania sinkings, new changes with women's suffrage, a world at war dragging America into conflict; and drug and alcohol addiction causing dozens of states to adopt prohibition.

Made in the USA
Coppell, TX
17 October 2021